Be the Reason You Thrive

Emotional Clarity, Honest Boundaries and Intentional Life

Fátima Y. Abreu Arellano

CARE TO VOICE

VOICE. LEAD. THRIVE.

To my birth land, **Venezuela**, with hope for a future of freedom and prosperity.

To my adoptive home, **Sydney, Australia**—thank you for welcoming me and opening doors to possibilities I once only dreamed of.

To **Alex, Luke, Teddy, family abroad and close friends**—your unconditional love is the compass that keeps me grounded and the fuel that keeps me moving forward.

And to **you, the reader**—thank you for choosing to walk this path of self-discovery alongside me. May these pages spark courage, clarity and the joy of becoming more fully yourself.

How It All Began

For years, I toyed with the idea of writing a book. I had memories, reflections and lessons swirling in my head, but every time I thought about putting them on paper, that little voice of doubt piped up: *Who would care about my story? What if I don't have anything worth saying?* For a long time, that voice won.

And yet, something inside kept tugging at me. On the surface, life looked good—I had a loving husband, a young family, good health and a career. But every so often, I felt a hollow space I couldn't explain. I tried to fill it with self-help books, yoga, fitness and various philosophies. Some of it helped, but the feeling always returned.

Here's the moment everything changed: I realised that what was missing wasn't another book to read or another philosophy to study—it was my own voice. I wasn't lacking information; I was longing for expression. I needed a way to give meaning to my experiences, to speak the truths I'd kept bottled up and to connect with others through something tangible.

That's when I discovered the power of storytelling. Speaking my truth—messy, raw and unfiltered—did more than ease the feeling. It lit a path. It helped me connect the dots, see patterns in my struggles and uncover lessons I didn't even know I'd lived. And when I began sharing those stories, I noticed something else: people leaned in. They saw themselves in my words. They didn't feel so alone—and neither did I.

That's why this book exists. It was born out of that missing piece, the hunger for something more authentic than surface-level fixes. Storytelling is the heartbeat of these pages—not just mine but hopefully ones that echo yours, too. Because when stories are shared, they build bridges. They whisper, *We're in this together. You're not alone.*

So let's keep it simple: think of this less like a lecture and more like a chat over coffee (or a glass of wine, depending on the day of the week). Sometimes I'll share a piece of my life. At other times, I'll nudge you to pause, reflect or try a small experiment that might shift your day. By the end, I hope you'll feel not only seen but also part of a bigger, braver conversation.

And here's what that conversation will look like:

This isn't about perfection. Together, we'll explore the big stuff we all face—self-doubt, confidence, boundaries, grief, burnout, joy, renewal—and find practical ways to navigate them with more honesty and less pressure. The book unfolds in three parts: first, uncovering how doubts and limiting beliefs shape our self-perception; second, rebuilding confidence and strengthening your inner voice; and finally, putting it all into practice with daily habits, boundaries set with grace, self-care that sticks and playful experiments that help you keep moving forward.

Now, I don't come to you as someone with all the answers (spoiler alert: you won't find a flawless guru here). My life has been a mix of brave leaps, clumsy mistakes, stubborn resilience and plenty of awkward laughter. But I've learnt—often the hard way—that honesty, boundaries and self-love aren't luxuries. They're essentials. That mix of vulnerability and determination is what shaped me, and it's what you'll find woven into these pages.

So, take this as your invitation—not to a perfect life but to a more authentic one. A life where change doesn't require dramatic leaps but instead begins with one brave step. A life where stories—yours and mine—light the way forward.

Because here's the truth: the life you're longing for isn't out there somewhere. It's already within you, quietly waiting. All it takes is the courage to listen.

If you're ready to laugh a little, reflect deeply and uncover the version of you that's been waiting all along—well, turn the page. Let's begin.

Contents

Part One

You Stick With What You Know, Even If It Hurts

Part One
You Stick With What You Know, Even If It Hurts

W e humans are funny creatures. We'll stay in jobs that drain us, play the "peacekeeper" in relationships until we're gritting our teeth or stick to routines that make us miserable—all because they feel safe. Change? Too risky. Familiar? Even if it's awful, at least we know the script. But those "safe" choices quietly box us in. This first section is about noticing where those patterns began and finding the guts to step past them—one small, honest move at a time.

And let's be clear: we don't cling to the familiar because we're foolish. We cling because it feels secure. When life is noisy, fast and full of people telling us who we "should" be, sticking with the known is tempting. It's like that pair of trackies you should've binned five years ago—holey, saggy, but somehow comforting. Most of us know the pull of "safe", even when it's quietly costing us. It's a shared human experience, a bond that unites us in our struggles.

Part one is about gently naming those patterns, seeing where they came from and loosening their grip without losing yourself. It's a journey of self-discovery. That ache you feel? It's not a weakness. It's a breadcrumb trail back to the kid in you who trusted, played and imagined without asking permission.

From there, we'll look at how life goes wobbly when one piece tilts out of balance. I will introduce you to the **CARE puzzle**, which is a harmonic combination of four pieces: **comfort, ambition, renewal and equilibrium.** It's not rocket science—just a way to notice the ripple effect when one part screams louder than the rest. Learn to balance them, and suddenly deadlines, family dramas and even Monday mornings become a bit easier to handle.

Then there are those sharp reactions that blindside you—the sting of a performance review, the snap in a tense conversation, the flush of a quick trigger. They're not random outbursts; they're your values raising their hands, asking to be seen. With a pause, a name and a breath, you can respond in ways that fit who you really are—not who old habits tell you to be. Think of it as emotional aikido: less flailing, more grace.

And of course, we can't ignore the noisy flatmate in all our heads—the mind that won't let go. Instead of trying to shut it up or fight it into silence, you'll learn how to set firm house rules. Boundaries for your own thoughts, spoken in a kind tone. A few micro-resets here, a CARE check-in there, and suddenly you've got space where both hope and doubt can live without taking over the whole lounge room.

Throughout this section, one thread remains constant: awareness first, compassion second and choice always. The goal isn't to reinvent yourself but to free the version of you that's been waiting in the wings. **With self-awareness, you hold the key to your own growth and transformation. It's a powerful tool that puts you in the driver's seat of your journey.**

So, if you've been clutching the familiar, even as it pinches, take this as your journey to ease your grip. Absolute comfort lives on the other side of honesty.

Let's take that first step together.

Chapter One

The Origins of Self-Doubt

Remember that kid you used to be? The one who ran barefoot through the grass, eyes wide with wonder, stuffed full of wild dreams and way too much sugar? You laughed at almost anything, made up games out of nothing and honestly believed you could grow up to be anything—astronaut, pop star, the neighbour's dog's personal trainer. Life felt big, and so did you. Back then, joy wasn't a puzzle to solve. You trusted yourself. Everything felt possible.

But somewhere along the way, something shifted.

Maybe it was a teacher, a parent or even a random stranger in the supermarket who decided you were "too much". Too loud. Too sensitive. Too imaginative. Apparently, life wasn't a fairytale (who knew?).

And that moment? It landed like a knot in your stomach—the first whisper that maybe, just maybe, you weren't enough as you were. So you started shrinking in little ways. You second-guessed yourself. You began editing the very things that once came naturally, *trying to fit into a world that seemed to reward blending in over standing out.*

Over the years, more voices piled on—friends, family, bosses, partners—each with their own script of who you "should" be. Most weren't cruel. Some meant well. But even well-meaning advice can turn into static when it drowns out your own voice.

And somewhere in the middle of all that noise, you forgot.

You forgot how to trust your gut.

You forgot how to follow your joy.

You forgot that your way—messy, bold, different—was never wrong.

Instead, you found yourself chasing the next shiny milestone: the job, the house, the title, the relationship. Each one looked like it might finally make you feel whole. And yet, deep down, there's still that quiet itch—the sense that something's missing, that you're not quite living as you.

I know that feeling well.

It took me years to unravel the web of expectations I'd wrapped myself in—years to stop asking for permission just to be me. Writing this book became part of that process. Not a lightning bolt of clarity but a journey through false starts, tears and far too many late-night drafts. Writing turned into my lifeline. My way back home to myself.

If you're sitting there thinking, yep, that's me—*good.* You're just on the path. And the path isn't meant to be perfect; it's meant to be walked.

So, let's go back together—back to the barefoot kid who already knew how to live wide open.

Intergenerational Baggage
(The Strange Lessons We Inherit)

If you've ever wondered why self-doubt sneaks under your skin so easily, you don't have to look far. Much of it comes from what has been passed down. Not just trauma or "big dramatic events" but the everyday echoes—little family sayings, cultural rules, unspoken expectations—that quietly ripple through generations and shape how we see ourselves.

Take the child of immigrants. Parents who've given up everything to start again in a new country pass down priceless lessons: be careful, don't waste opportunities, honour your roots. All important. All wise. But they can also feel heavy. Suddenly, choosing a career that isn't "safe" or loving someone outside expectations comes with a side order of guilt. Freedom feels selfish, even when it's just human.

When I moved from South America to Australia 24 years ago, I quickly discovered that even ordinary things can teach you about a country's values. On our very first morning in Sydney, jet-lagged and half alive, I was woken by a low rumble outside. We pulled back the curtains, and there it was: a garbage truck. But not just any truck. This one had a robotic arm that gracefully picked up the bin, tipped it and placed it back down, as if pouring a glass of wine.

Back home, rubbish collection was sweaty, manual, hard labour. Watching that robotic arm blew my mind. It wasn't just about efficiency—it was a statement. A reminder that there are always different ways to solve the same problem, and how a society handles even its trash says something about how it treats people, honours labour and imagines progress.

That truck became my first unexpected lesson in belonging: *sometimes the little things are the big things.*

And intergenerational baggage works a bit like that garbage truck, too. Some things are lifted and carried forward with care, while others—old beliefs, outdated roles—are dumped on us whether we asked for them or not. Take the legacy of being a woman. Today, we celebrate women smashing glass ceilings, but not that long ago, the message was clear: *be pure, be supportive, don't rock the boat.* Women who dared to dream bigger often paid the price—balancing ambition with judgement at home, at work and everywhere in between.

Religion reinforced the mould too. I attended an all-girls Catholic school in the 1980s, and looking back, it's remarkable how much it shaped us. We were taught to knit and sew (as if that was our life's destiny), but we learnt almost nothing about our own bodies, independence or emotional wellbeing. If you didn't fit the mould, you weren't quirky—you were rebellious. Independence wasn't encouraged; it was seen as a threat.

And the boys? They got a different script: *be strong, be stoic, provide.* Vulnerability was weakness. Tears were off-limits. Many grew up disconnected from their feelings, expected to perform strength with a straight face and a silent heart.

For others raised in unstable homes, the lessons were harsher. Survival meant resilience. Sometimes that grit became fuel for greatness; other times, it left scars. Either way, self-doubt often takes root in the gaps where love or safety should have been.

The truth is, we all carry some form of baggage. Some of it's heavy. Some of it's quiet. Some of it we don't notice until it pops up in the weirdest places—like in the job we go for (or don't), the way we swallow our ideas in meetings or who we let close enough to matter.

The stories we inherit aren't all bad. Some are full of wisdom and strength. But they're not the whole truth either. *The real work is sorting through the hand-me-downs: keeping what still fits, tossing what's outdated and deciding what belongs to the past. That's how we create new legacies.* Not perfect ones, but ones built on awareness, compassion and the freedom to be who we really are.

Coping: The Shields That Become Walls

Once you start to notice how much other people shape you—the offhand comments, the rules, the expectations—one thing becomes obvious: *those influences don't just pass by like a tram. They seep in.* They colour how you see yourself, and they quietly steer the choices you make. Everyone's take is different. Your history, your values, the messes you've survived—they all shape how you cope. Over time, we invent strategies (sometimes clever, sometimes ridiculous) to carve out a space where we feel safe, seen and, ideally, a bit less freaked out.

Here's the catch: the very things that kept us afloat can turn into anchors. A shield that once protected you can become a wall. *Without realising it, we trade freedom for familiarity and growth for comfort.*

One way this manifests is depersonalisation. Fancy name, weird feeling. Think of it as your brain's emergency exit when emotions get too loud. Instead of feeling everything full-on, you step back—like watching your life through a fogged window or a poorly filmed documentary. Your body feels not-quite-you. Colours go flat, and sensations become distant.

For some, it's lifesaving in a brutal moment; for others, it becomes a way of living by accident.

I found out how that works in the worst possible way. When my mum got COVID in 2020, everything went sideways. Travel bans meant I couldn't be there. I FaceTimed her every day, trying to read the screen for signs she was okay, counting down insurance days like some terrible stopwatch. It was dread, phone calls, forms and a constant sense of helplessness. Then one Sunday, her doctor said, "It is done." For a beat, my brain refused to take it in. Then it hit—my brother had stepped out for a priest; she took her last breath alone. I still see that moment too clearly.

I swung into practical mode. I helped my brother from across the ocean—with the paperwork, organising the release and finding a cremation urn—guiding him step by step while holding myself together by sheer stubbornness. We had a small ceremony attended by just five people. I watched her face one last time through a screen. After that, I cried for weeks and barely slept for months. Sleeping pills took the edge off, yes—but they also dulled joy, turned laughter into a memory and left me floating through life a little hollowed out. I wasn't present so much as buffered.

That numbness kept me going, but it wasn't living. Eventually, I realised that hiding inside a quieter version of myself wasn't protection—it was avoidance. I had to let the pain in, even if it broke me for a while. From that hard, honest place came a lesson I won't forget: ***to feel alive again, you have to walk through your most profound sadness, not around it.***

Pain taught me another thing, too. When we've been hurt, we tighten the reins. We tell ourselves we're being sensible—protecting our hearts—but slowly that sensible guarding becomes control. We build little fortresses: rules, micro-managing, doing more, all so we feel safe. The problem is that walls keep out both the cold and the warmth. Creativity, mess, connection—all the good stuff—gets shut out with the bad.

So yeah, coping strategies? They're brilliant. They keep us upright when the world shakes. But they're also sneaky. If we don't notice them, they become the very thing that stops us from living the life we actually want.

The Control Game ...

When life feels shaky, many of us reach for control. We micro-manage conversations, steer relationships and try to script the ending before the story has even begun. On paper, it makes sense: control equals predictability, predictability equals safety. But in practice? It backfires. Instead of protecting the connection, control suffocates it. It shatters trust, leaving you standing alone, wondering why everyone else has pulled away. And the cruel irony? The tighter you grip, the messier it gets. Chaos doesn't leave—in fact, you've just invited it to move in.

Now, when we picture control, most of us imagine the obvious: the bossy manager, the friend who has to "fix" everything. But control often wears quieter clothes. It slips in under the radar, and it can come from either side of the table.

Ask yourself: Do you get twitchy when you can't predict someone's reaction? Do you "just check" a colleague's work, drop in advice no one asked for or quietly panic when plans change without your say? Perhaps you use guilt to nudge people, or you withhold affection until they fall back in line. Sometimes it's not dramatic at all—it's keeping a silent scorecard of favours and slights, as if relationships were bank accounts.

But what if you're on the receiving end? Perhaps you hold back your honest opinions to avoid conflict, tiptoe around someone else's moods or feel guilty about making choices without consulting another person first. Perhaps your boundaries are brushed aside, or your world is slowly narrowed so that one voice dominates and others are shut out.

The thing is, control isn't always loud. It shows up in the little moments we excuse or overlook. That's why noticing matters. *So pause and ask yourself: Are you the one holding the reins too tightly ... or are you letting someone else have them for you?*

Either way, you can't change what you won't name. And you can't break free from a pattern you refuse to see.

Enough Is Never Enough ...

Here's the sneaky twist: control isn't always about bossing people around. Sometimes it hides in what we cling to. When life feels uncertain, we don't just try to manage people—we try to manage our sense of safety. So we surround ourselves with more. More things. More connections. More proof that we're okay. It feels different from control, but deep down, it's the same craving: *the need to fill that gap inside with something we can hold onto.*

Excess. That coping mechanism that whispers, *If I just get one more thing, then I'll finally feel enough.* More clothes, more friends, more "life-changing" retreats, more certificates for the LinkedIn wall of fame. (Seriously, some of us could open a museum of half-finished online courses.) And it's not just personal anymore. It feels like we're all strapped onto a cultural conveyor belt heading for the checkout, whether we want to or not.

Take social media. Every platform is the same circus, just a different tent. On Facebook, you so much as blink at something, and the algorithm decides it's your new life mission. Look at a gadget for three seconds? Suddenly, you're being stalked by 47 versions of it. Before you know it, you're thinking, *Maybe I do need a glow-in-the-dark avocado slicer to reach my full potential.*

And yep, I fell for it once. Bought a "miracle cream" that promised to make me look 20 again. It didn't. What it did do was give me an allergic reaction that made me look puffier, older, like my own bad decisions had just punched me. We've all been there—dancing that ridiculous waltz of neediness and nonsense.

So how do you know the difference between a genuine need and an emotional "must-have"? Usually, it comes down to timing. A genuine need solves a problem right now—like replacing your broken phone or buying groceries because, well, you'd like to eat this week. An emotional "must-have" is the thing that excites or comforts you in the moment, promising a better life without delivering much.

Here's the quick test: if you wait a week, will it still matter? If yes, it's a need. If no, it's just your emotions taking your credit card on a little shopping spree.

And maybe that's the real question: ***How much of what you're chasing is about what you actually need—and how much is just you trying to fill a gap that was never meant to be filled with stuff in the first place?***

Because if "enough" has never really been about more ... what has it been about all along?

Bringing It All Together: Key Takeaways

So what do we do with all this? We start by remembering: *You were never broken. You don't need to earn your worth.* Much of what you believe about yourself came from other people's stories—family scripts, cultural rules, workplace expectations. Some served you. Some didn't.

The primary focus of this chapter isn't to erase the past but to see it clearly. To notice where self-doubt came from, and how those old coping strategies still play out in meetings, relationships or late-night scrolls through ads for jobs you don't even want.

And here's the good news: *You have the power to choose again. You can keep what empowers you—resilience, care and cultural pride—and release what doesn't—silencing your voice, shrinking your dreams and grasping for control.*

True comfort isn't in fitting the mould. It's in stepping beyond it. It's in remembering the fearless child you once were and choosing to live as your whole, messy, joyful self.

That's where the next version of your career, relationships and life is waiting.

ARRIVING IN SYDNEY

MY BROTHER JAVIER

INTERGENERATIONAL BAGGAGE

THE REAL WORK IS
SORTING THROUGH THE
HAND-ME-DOWNS.
KEEPING WHAT STILL FITS,
TOSSING WHAT'S OUTDATED
AND DECIDING WHAT
BELONGS TO THE PAST.
THAT'S HOW WE CREATE
NEW LEGACIES.

Fatima

Chapter Two

When One Piece Breaks, the Whole Puzzle Feels Wrong

We're wonderfully complex creatures—part organs and bones, part feelings and habits, all tangled together in a way that's uniquely ours. What makes you different from me isn't just one thing—it could be a moment, a memory or even an experience. That's why creating one "perfect formula" for everyone is about as likely as finding the holy grail.

Still, there are patterns. While we're all unique, most of us share some common elements that, when they come together, give life a sense of harmony. And when one breaks, the whole puzzle feels off. You might not even notice at first—you just know something isn't right, like an itch you can't scratch.

In this chapter, I want to share my take on four big pieces we all seem to carry—parts of ourselves that quietly (or sometimes loudly) push us forward, shape our choices, and colour our relationships with both ourselves and others. I'm not here to oversimplify the human experience but to explore how these pieces connect, influence us, and sometimes turn life into either a beautiful song or a bit of a mess.

So, come along on this little adventure with me. Let's figure out which piece in your own inner puzzle might need a bit of nurturing, so the rest can fall into harmony and lift your whole existence. This chapter is about those pieces—the ones I call the **CARE puzzle**.

The CARE Puzzle

Picture your life as a four-piece puzzle—simple in shape but powerful in meaning. Each piece represents an essential part of you. When all four come together, they form the picture of who you are at your best. Together, they spell **CARE**—because when we tend to these areas, we genuinely care for ourselves.

- **Comfort (C):** Your safe haven—where you feel grounded, supported, at ease.
- **Ambition (A):** The fire that drives you forward—your purpose, dreams and goals.
- **Renewal (R):** Your energy, creativity and health—the fuel that keeps you moving.
- **Equilibrium (E):** Your inner balance—the calm centre that steadies you when life tilts.

None of these pieces works in isolation. They're like instruments in a band. When they're in tune, you get music. When one's off, it doesn't matter how well the others play—something will sound wrong.

When One Piece Slips

Think back to a time when one corner of your life felt off. Maybe it was work—a boss who drained your energy or a project that kept you awake at 3 am. Or perhaps it was something smaller, like an unresolved argument or even the nagging guilt of not getting to the gym for weeks.

The funny thing is, these aren't "small" at all. One loose thread can unravel the whole jumper. A bad day at work can easily bleed into snapping at your partner. Your lack of sleep leaves you feeling foggy during the meeting. Your shaky confidence colours the way you see yourself. Suddenly, it's not just "one thing"—it's everything.

And then someone says, "Just be present! Don't think about it!" As if you can mute your brain with one click. If only it were that simple.

Some people do manage to compartmentalise like Jedi masters, calmly setting aside their lightsaber and moving on. For the rest of us? It's like the dark side. The harder you try to shove the feeling down, the stronger it gets—fuelled by anger, frustration, self-doubt—until it spills into everything else.

I've been there—more than once. The days when life feels like a long tunnel with no light in sight, only to realise later that the "switch" was right beside me but I was too busy catastrophising to notice. It's like living under your own weather forecast: "Expect 100% chance of drama, with heavy patches of self-criticism."

In those moments, I'd try patch fixes. A new outfit. A stricter routine. A bit of emotional autopilot. They helped for about as long as a cup of instant noodles does. Real change came when I started asking: ***Which piece of my CARE puzzle is out of balance, and how is it affecting the others?***

The PIG Effect

When I signed up for a voluntary subject called *Sociology* at uni back home, I imagined hours of deep discussions and life-changing ideas. Instead, on day one, the lecturer announced we'd be learning about something called "The PIG Effect". I had no idea what that meant, but I was intrigued—partly because the name made me wonder if breakfast was included.

To explain, he showed us an old film in English—at the time, I understood English about as well as a goldfish understands algebra. The film was so dated it felt like watching an old Mr Bean sketch: no words, lots of exaggerated drama and the sinking suspicion that something ridiculous was about to happen.

The story went like this: A man in a MINI Cooper, already rattled by the news of rising unemployment and new taxes, speeds through town in a rush to get to work. Suddenly, a boy on a bicycle swerves in front of him, shouts "PIG!" (somewhere between insult and warning), then vanishes. The driver, furious, hits the accelerator to chase him—only to turn the corner and slam straight into a herd of actual pigs.

The moral of the story? Sometimes "PIG!" isn't an insult. It's a warning. Though in this case, it was more like a slapstick prophecy straight out of Mr Bean.

Peter's Puzzle

Now, let's climb into Peter-the-driver's head for a second and check out his **CARE puzzle** in action.

- **Comfort (C):** Rattled. The news has poked at his sense of security. He's suddenly wondering if his job is next on the chopping block. Unease grows.

- **Ambition (A):** Under pressure. He's late for work, worried his boss will doubt his commitment. Anxiety fuels his urgency.

- **Renewal (R):** Shot. Instead of calming himself, his energy is pouring straight into frustration. His jaw is clenched, his shoulders stiff; his irritation is humming like static.

- **Equilibrium (E):** Gone. Anger has taken the wheel. One red light or slow driver away from a meltdown, he feels like the whole world is against him.

See how it unravels? One shaky piece—his comfort—sets off a domino effect. Ambition becomes panic. Renewal becomes rage. Equilibrium collapses altogether. That's how it works for all of us: ***When one piece wobbles, the others don't just politely stay put. They tumble right along with it.***

Spotting Your Wobbly Piece

The tricky part is that when life feels "off", we often don't know which piece of the puzzle is the culprit. It's like staring at a half-built jigsaw and thinking, *Something's missing, but where?*

Here's a quick way to check in with yourself.

- Ask: Do I feel safe and grounded at this moment? **(Comfort)**

- Ask: Am I feeling motivated and purposeful, or am I stuck in a state of pressure? **(Ambition)**

- Ask: Is my energy being renewed, or am I running on fumes? **(Renewal)**

- Ask: Am I emotionally steady, or are my moods running the show? **(Equilibrium)**

Even just pausing to ask these questions can reveal which piece is out of sync. Sometimes it's obvious. At other times, the real crack lies beneath the surface—stress at work (ambition) might actually be about feeling unsafe (comfort).

And here's the key: once you notice a wobble, resist the urge to jump straight into reactive mode. You know the drill—retail therapy, snapping at someone, overworking, pouring another wine or rearranging the pantry at midnight. Those quick fixes are like slapping sticky tape on a cracked wall: they cover things up for a while, but they don't fix the foundation.

Instead, stop. Breathe. Look for clarity. *Ask yourself: What's really being threatened here?* Which piece of my puzzle needs attention, not a distraction? That moment of pause can be the difference between spiralling further and gently nudging yourself back towards balance.

And this part's on you. No one else can crawl inside your head and figure out which puzzle piece needs sorting. Your champions (support network) can help you, yes—but the responsibility to look honestly at yourself, to search for the piece that's wobbling, belongs to you. You can either continue functioning in reactive mode, letting old habits drive you, or you can take ownership, pause and choose the action that actually repairs the puzzle.

Champions, Not Clichés

When your puzzle pieces are sliding around and you can't see clearly, champions are the ones who help you put the picture back together, not by solving it for you but by standing with you while you untangle it yourself.

They're the friends, mentors or even pets who don't toss you a "Hakuna Matata" cliché and walk away. Instead, they help you slow down, breathe and notice which piece of your CARE puzzle actually needs attention. Is it your comfort that's been rattled? Your ambition running wild? Is your renewal running on empty? Or your equilibrium tipping over?

Champions don't dismiss your feelings; they hold up the mirror gently so that you can spot the cracks. They make you feel safe enough to admit where you're wobbling and strong enough to start rebuilding.

And sometimes, your champions aren't the people you expect. Sometimes, they're your kids.

One night, while playing our favourite card game, *family roast*, my nine-year-old surprised me. One card asked: "What is something you've never told this family?" He remembered an incident at school months earlier, when an educator thought he'd been rude after she abruptly took his iPad. What she hadn't seen was that he wasn't sneaking a game—he was saving a friend's phone number.

I'd gone to the school at the time to hear both sides, explained our preference that he be spoken to first before things were taken away, and the educator eventually apologised. For me, the matter ended there. But clearly, this was not the case for him.

That night, after he read the card, he looked at me and said, "Mum, you made me proud that day. You didn't just react—you listened to her side and my side. You understood why I reacted, and that made me feel safe."

His words floored me. In that moment, he wasn't the one

being championed—I was. He reminded me of something bigger: just as others can shake or steady pieces of our **CARE puzzle**, we inevitably shape theirs too—through our words, reactions, even our silences. We live in an intricately woven web where every gesture sends ripples we can't always see.

The truth is, we rarely know the whole story of where someone is coming from. Our view is always through the narrow lens of our own experience. But when we pause, step outside ourselves and look through another's eyes, something shifts. We begin to see that even our smallest choices can either mend or fracture someone's inner world.

Once you see that connection, you can't unsee it anymore. That's why finding (and being) a champion matters. They're more than just pleasant company—they're the people who help you steady the puzzle when it wobbles. They clear the fog so you can see what's really going on, and they remind you—sometimes more than you can remind yourself—that your voice, your feelings, and your worth are real and important.

Asking for Help

Let's be real—sometimes the people who love you most simply won't know how to guide you back to the light. Not because they don't care but because carrying that responsibility can be too heavy for them. That's where reaching out for professional help makes all the difference.

Needing help means you're taking ownership. Seeking support isn't weakness—it's courage in action. Whether you're experiencing grief, struggling to find balance or just craving clarity, reaching out isn't a desperate last resort; it's a wise investment in yourself.

And here's the thing—you don't have to wait until you've hit rock bottom. Think of it as the mental health version of a routine check-up: something that keeps your puzzle strong before any cracks widen.

Internal Validation vs External Approval

Not long ago, I found myself caught in a quiet tug-of-war between two heavyweights: "internal validation" and "external approval". I knew the terms, but I didn't fully grasp how differently they shaped how I measured my worth. Both appear in our lives, but they don't carry the same weight when it comes to building genuine, lasting confidence.

This became crystal clear when I connected it back to the **CARE puzzle**. Each piece—comfort, ambition, renewal, equilibrium—represents a core element of wellbeing. Understanding whether we're driven by internal validation or by chasing external approval doesn't just change the way we live; it's the key to keeping the whole puzzle balanced and genuinely ours.

So, what's the difference?

- **Internal validation** is when your sense of worth comes from within. You trust your own judgement, values and achievements without needing a constant round of applause.

- **External approval** is when your worth hangs in the praise, recognition or acceptance of others—like needing a scoreboard to prove you're winning.

The **CARE puzzle** works the same way. All four pieces matter, but the quality of each piece depends heavily on which motivator is steering you. If you're driven by internal validation, the puzzle feels solid. If you're chasing external approval, the puzzle looks fine for a while—but one bad review or one withheld compliment, and it wobbles.

Let's see how both interact with our inner puzzle.

CARE Puzzle:
Internal Validation vs External Approval

CARE Element	Internal Validation	External Approval
Comfort	Feeling content because your actions align with your values and you know your worth.	Feeling "at ease" only when others approve of your choices.
Ambition	Pursuing goals that matter to you, regardless of public recognition.	Setting goals mainly to impress or match societal expectations.
Renewal	Recharging because you believe you deserve rest, joy, and restoration.	Only allowing yourself rest when you've earned praise or recognition.
Equilibrium	Creating balance that reflects your priorities.	Trying to balance based on what others expect you to prioritise.

Here's a simple analogy: think of the **CARE puzzle** as a house. Internal validation is the foundation—solid, unseen, carrying all the weight. External approval is the paint—it makes things look good, but without a foundation, the whole house will eventually collapse.

My Own Tug-of-War

Life tests all of us in ways we don't see coming. Loss, change and even the quiet weight of everyday struggles can tip the balance. And in those moments, it's tempting to hide behind a smile or pretend we can carry it all alone. However, the truth is that sometimes the bravest thing we can do is admit we can't.

For years, I measured myself almost entirely by external approval. My corporate identity became my safety blanket. I was capable, specialised, respected—but boxed in. A quiet voice inside whispered that I wanted more—that I wanted to write, to share, to help others find their own strength. But another, louder voice snapped back:

You don't have anything worth sharing.
Nobody will relate to your experiences.
You're not a professional writer—don't be ridiculous.
Stick to what you were trained to do. Forever.

Those thoughts, fuelled by the need for approval, kept me stuck.

It took courage, stubbornness and a lot of self-reflection to quiet those voices. Slowly, I began giving more credit to my inner compass—trusting my own validation rather than seeking permission from others. I let myself dream, explore and create.

And now, here you are—reading this book. Proof that sometimes the loudest battle is the one happening in your own head.

Your Turn

So, what's your dream? The project, idea or passion you keep tucking away because some imaginary critic might not approve?

Here's the secret: *The "perfect" time will never arrive unless you make it. Internal validation is choosing to start today— not because the world claps but because you know it matters.*

Bringing It All Together: Key Takeaways

When we recognise how connected we all are, it invites a bigger question: *What am I bringing into the shared space?* If your confidence rests only on other people's praise, it disappears the moment that praise dries up. But when you learn to value yourself from the inside out, you show up with more honesty and steadiness. You give without expecting rewards, and you receive without bending yourself into shapes for approval.

That's when your presence becomes real, grounded and meaningful. Not another puzzle piece forcing itself to fit but one that belongs naturally in the bigger picture we're all creating together.

So how do you carry this forward? Start with the puzzle itself. The **CARE** framework—*comfort, ambition, renewal and equilibrium*—isn't just an idea; it's a practical way of checking in with yourself. Notice which piece wobbles first when life feels heavy. Pay attention before the ripple spreads everywhere.

Anchor yourself in internal validation, because it sustains. External approval will come and go, but the steadiness you build inside lasts. Surround yourself with champions—the people who remind you of your strength without rushing in to fix you. Protect your energy with acts of self-care—even the small ones that signal safety to your nervous system. And remember: *Your choices don't stop with you. They ripple outward, shaping the puzzles of other people as well.*

And if you find yourself slipping, reach out. Asking for help is not failure—it's courage. It's owning your puzzle and choosing to keep building it strong.

Your task now is simple but not easy: pause, notice and make a choice. *What piece of your puzzle needs attention today? What small step could bring it back into balance?* And most importantly, *What energy are you letting into the shared space we all live in?*

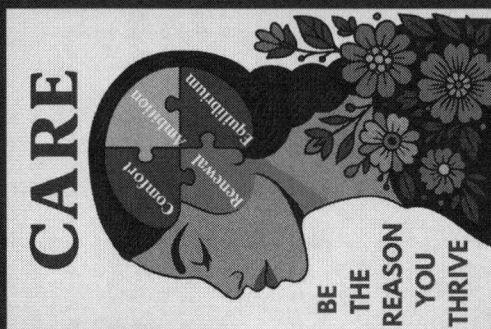

WHEN ONE PIECE WOBBLES, THE OTHERS DON'T JUST POLITELY STAY PUT. THEY TUMBLE RIGHT ALONG WITH IT.

Fatima

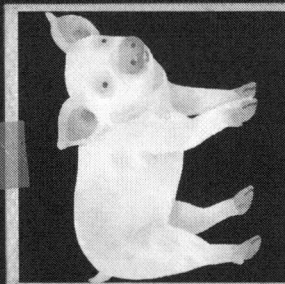

Chapter Three

Discover What's Behind Your Triggers

Sometimes we're set off by people, passing moments, certain behaviours or even the way something looks. Out of nowhere, we're frustrated, upset or confused—and left wondering why. Most of the time, the real cause lies just beneath the surface, out of view.

Have you noticed that lately? A comment that lingers longer than it should. A tone that tightens your shoulders. If you pause and look a little closer—not to judge yourself but to get curious—you'll often find a pattern. That pause is where clarity begins: *it's the difference between reacting on autopilot and responding with intent.*

Let me take you to a familiar scene. I'm a lifelong *Back to the Future* fan (teenage crush on Michael J. Fox fully acknowledged). Remember Marty McFly and his nemesis, Biff Tannen? There's that classic hook: Biff sneers, "Are you a chicken?"—and Marty explodes. Three words and he's off, charging into trouble he isn't ready for. It's funny on screen, but it's also a neat reminder: a tiny cue can unlock an immense feeling and nudge us into choices we didn't mean to make. If a single word can send Marty spinning, it's no wonder small cues rattle us too. The difference is knowing what they're bumping into.

Beneath those spikes of feeling sit your values—the quiet drivers of what helps you feel safe, purposeful and steady. I call the way they work together your **CARE puzzle: comfort, ambition, renewal and equilibrium.** When life lines up with these, you feel like yourself. When it doesn't, friction shows up: you second-guess, tense up or go numb.

There's also a well-researched lens that helps us make sense of this: **self-determination theory (SDT)**. It suggests that, underneath our goals and daily choices, three basic psychological needs power motivation and wellbeing: **autonomy (a sense of choice), competence (a sense of capability)** and **relatedness (a sense of connection)**. When these needs are met, life feels aligned; when they're blocked, tension rises—and triggers get louder.

CARE and SDT fit together naturally.

- **Comfort ↔ relatedness**: trust, safety, belonging
- **Ambition ↔ autonomy + competence**: room to decide, room to grow
- **Renewal ↔ intrinsic interest**: activities that restore energy and joy
- **Equilibrium ↔ alignment**: balance so no part needs to shout

When a moment jolts you—a look, a phrase, an email—you can ask, gently: *Which part of my CARE puzzle was nudged? Which SDT need felt blocked for me?* That simple curiosity turns a trigger into information. And with information, you can choose your next move—calmer, clearer, more you.

As you move through this chapter, you'll get to know these pieces more deeply—how they shape your reactions, what they reveal about your needs, and how tuning into them can transform the way you experience yourself and others. Think of this as an invitation to slow down, observe and reconnect with what truly drives you.

What Really Matters?
A Deep Dive Into Your Values

Let's say I've decided to be the willing guinea pig in this experiment called self-awareness. If someone could peek inside my brain, they'd find a half-finished puzzle made of emotional Post-it notes, snack crumbs and a few hard-earned life lessons. That puzzle? It's called CARE—my personal framework for making sense of how I show up in the world.

And because I'm brave, bored or just oddly committed to personal growth, I've volunteered to take you through the values that sit inside me. Spoiler alert: they're simple, they're honest and they keep me from losing my mind.

Comfort Trust Stability Belonging	**Ambition** Learning Achievement Fairness
Renewal Joy Rest Energy	**Equilibrium** Flexibility Mindfulness Balance

My Inner CARE Puzzle and Values

In everyday life, my CARE puzzle acts like a quiet compass—it doesn't shout, but it keeps me steady when things get messy.

Comfort is about trust, stability and belonging. When those are in place, I feel grounded and calm. I can listen without defensiveness, speak with patience and hold my ground when something matters. For instance, when I trust others, I can delegate or ask for help without fear. And when I feel like I belong, I show up with more confidence, even in challenging conversations.

Ambition brings purpose. It's made up of learning, achievement and fairness—values that push me to grow without judging others along the way. They remind me to stay curious, to seek understanding before opinion. When I act from fairness, I'm able to respect different views and keep discussions balanced instead of tense. Ambition helps me speak up when something feels off, but I do so from purpose, not ego.

Renewal and equilibrium are the glue that hold everything together. Renewal is about rest, energy and joy—the reminder that I don't have to be "on" all the time. It's what keeps me from running on empty and allows me to bring my best self to the people around me.

Equilibrium is about balance, helping me flow with life rather than fight it. When plans change or someone's mood shifts, I can adapt. Together, these values keep me from burning out and help me stay present instead of pressured.

When Life Rearranges Your Values

Have you ever had a moment when everything familiar—your language, your comfort zone, even your sense of direction—just disappeared overnight? When simple things, like buying milk or asking for help, felt like reading a map upside down in a storm?

Those moments hit deeper than we expect. They make us stop and ask: *Are my values still relevant in this new reality? Do they still fit?*

Sometimes the answer surprises us. Some values hold firm like anchors; others need reshaping—not because we've lost ourselves but because we're growing. And that's okay. Updating a few values for your wellbeing doesn't mean abandoning your essence. It just means evolving it.

My Wake-Up Call in Australia

Change has a funny way of testing our values in real time. It's one thing to talk about growth and flexibility—it's another to live it. Sometimes, life doesn't just nudge your values; it shakes them up like a snow globe and waits to see where everything lands. You think you know what matters most until a big move, a new culture or an unexpected challenge holds up a mirror and asks, "Are you still sure?" For me, that mirror appeared the moment I stepped off a plane in Australia.

I had one of those "who even am I anymore?" moments during my first year in Australia. Actually, I had several. And let me tell you—it wasn't the shiny, sun-soaked beginning I had imagined.

When I first landed in Sydney, I thought I was starting a bold new chapter. Plot twist: *it was more like a rollercoaster without a seatbelt.* I'd left behind everything—family, friends, language and the comfort of knowing how things worked. My husband found a job quickly (good for him), but I could barely speak English. Trying to get a job felt like showing up to a job interview in invisible ink.

Meanwhile, Sydney was out there being stunning—and expensive—and I was waking up most mornings thinking, *Do I really have to get out of bed today?*

My comfort and ambition puzzle pieces were having a full-blown identity crisis. I desperately missed home and began to doubt whether this "new life" was worth it. But things back home were worsening—political unrest, growing military control, human rights slipping away. Going back wasn't an option.

So, I decided: fine—if life was going to test me, Sydney would be my training ground.

My first teacher? The supermarket. I practised English by

translating cereal boxes, sang along to songs with a dictionary and made friends with neighbours (a big deal for someone who is terrified of small talk).

Eventually, I saved enough to enrol in a human resources TAFE diploma course. My first day, all I understood was "good morning" and "see you tomorrow". The rest was a blur of confusion and panic. But I stuck with it. Five years later, I was in MBA lectures at the University of Technology Sydney (UTS)—the same person who once learnt grammar from milk cartons. Looking back, every small step added a piece back to my CARE puzzle. It wasn't easy or tidy—but it was mine.

Looking back, that season of uncertainty taught me something I couldn't have learnt any other way: growth rarely feels graceful while it's happening. It's awkward, humbling and often wrapped in self-doubt. But every stumble and small win in those early Sydney days shaped a stronger, more grounded version of me—someone who understands that comfort doesn't always mean safety and discomfort doesn't always mean danger. Sometimes, it's just life's way of showing you what you're truly capable of. And maybe that's the point: the moments that shake us the most often end up becoming the ones that align us back to who we really are.

When Your Values Evolve

Sometimes, adapting your values is the healthiest thing you can do—especially when life pushes you in a new direction. What matters most is *staying connected to your essence*: the things that make you feel whole, cared for and grounded.

Knowing your true values—whether fairness, belonging, purpose or something else—allows you to grow without losing yourself. It's like updating your home's furniture without tearing down the house. You keep the foundation; you just make it fit your new season of life.

When Your CARE Puzzle Doesn't Match the Room

But what happens when your values don't quite fit the world—or the people—around you? That's when it gets tricky. You might feel uneasy, defensive, like something is off.

Once you notice the mismatch, you can make conscious choices: *communicate, set boundaries or even shift your environment.*

It's not about forcing others to share your values. It's about protecting the ones that help you thrive—while leaving enough space for growth, understanding and connection.

When you realise your values aren't landing in the space you're in, it can stir a mix of confusion and clarity all at once. On one hand, you start to see yourself more clearly; on the other, you might feel torn between fitting in and staying true to who you are. That's where reflection becomes powerful. It's not about judging the people or the situation—it's about noticing what's happening inside you. Because every uncomfortable moment, every emotional tug, is a breadcrumb leading you back to your core values. And the only way to follow that trail is to pause long enough to listen.

Name one situation that felt "off" this week. *Which value was nudged? What's one boundary or conversation that would restore alignment?*

Pause. Reflect. Realign:
Are Your Values Keeping Up?

Have you ever caught yourself thinking, *Why do I always go back to that memory?*

Or, *Why did that one moment hit me so hard?*

That's not random.

Psychologist Dan McAdams suggests that we all have an inner storyteller—one who is constantly weaving our experiences into a bigger story about who we are, where we've been and where we're going.

When you feel a sense of discomfort or unease in an interaction—whether it's frustration, tension or just that "off" feeling—it's often a sign that one of your values has been bumped, challenged or ignored. These moments aren't just emotional reactions; they're gentle invitations to pause and look inward.

Your values are like internal guideposts that help you feel grounded and respected. So when something feels off, instead of brushing it aside, try asking yourself: *What value of mine was touched here?* Was it your need for honesty, respect, connection or autonomy? Understanding this is the first step to reclaiming your clarity.

Practical reflection helps move you from reaction to awareness. Ask yourself questions like:

Why did that interaction feel nourishing—or draining?

Why do I feel misaligned right now?

These "why" prompts shine a light on the need behind the discomfort. Maybe you admire someone because they live out a value you want to strengthen—or you feel irritation because they're challenging a value you hold dear. When a decision feels hard, it might be because you're torn between two values: *one that feels safe and another that's calling you to grow.*

Sometimes the solution is to restore a value through a boundary, a conversation or a small act of courage. Other times, growth means evolving your values to match who you're becoming—either way, asking "why" is how you reconnect with your CARE puzzle and return to emotional alignment.

Cognitive dissonance theory helps explain why this matters. When your actions clash with your core beliefs or values, you experience a mental tug-of-war called *dissonance*. It shows up as discomfort, guilt, shame or confusion—and your brain naturally tries to reduce it by changing the behaviour or rationalising it away.

But when the value in question is one of your non-negotiables—the principles that define who you are—the dissonance hits harder. These are the moments when your inner alarm goes off, saying, *Something here isn't okay with who I am.* The more essential the value, the louder that alarm. That's your cue to realign—to speak up, adjust course or step away—so you can find your balance again.

When that alarm rings, ask: *Do I repair this (boundary/ conversation) or release it (step away)?*

What You Won't Bend On

Non-negotiable values are the beliefs that live right at the core of who you are. They're not preferences or "nice-to-haves"— they're the emotional anchors that hold you steady when life gets messy. Think of them as your personal red lines: when they're crossed, something inside you jolts. You feel that sharp sense of discomfort, guilt or even shame, because these values touch the deepest part of your identity.

They're usually shaped by lived experience—moments that taught you what really matters. Maybe it's honesty, because you've seen what happens when the truth is twisted. Perhaps it's loyalty, fairness or personal freedom. Whatever yours are, they quietly guide how you behave, make decisions and draw boundaries. They shape how you show up in the world—and what you expect from others in return.

What makes these values non-negotiable is that compromising them feels like betraying yourself. When they're violated—by someone else or even by your own choices—you feel it instantly, like an internal alarm going off. These values aren't rigid rules; they're steady foundations. You don't hold on to them because you're stubborn—you hold on because letting them go would mean losing a piece of who you are.

In relationships, at work and in everyday choices, honouring your non-negotiables builds something powerful: self-respect. It's what allows you to say "no" without guilt and "yes" without hesitation. Knowing your red lines helps you understand your triggers, set healthier boundaries and make authentic decisions rather than reactive ones.

But here's where it gets even more meaningful: when you start sharing your values out loud. Communicating what truly matters to you—with friends, family or colleagues—sets clear expectations about how you want to be treated and how you intend to treat others. It's not about creating a conflict-free life. It's about developing relationships rooted in honesty and respect.

When people understand your boundaries—whether around time, trust, honesty or personal space—they're more likely to meet you where you are. And when conflicts do happen, that shared understanding changes everything. Instead of reacting with confusion or frustration, both sides can pause and think, *Ah, this might be touching one of their core values.* That kind of awareness fosters empathy, better communication and a smoother path forward.

Ultimately, expressing your non-negotiables isn't about being demanding—it's about being real. ***When people know what you stand for, relationships become less about guesswork and more about genuine connection. And that's where respect, trust and understanding truly begin.***

It's Not About You—It's Their Projection

It's a strange thing, isn't it? With some people, connection just clicks—you talk easily, laugh naturally and build trust without effort. But with others, even the simplest interaction can feel awkward, tense or strangely heavy. It might happen in a meeting, a collaboration or a casual chat at work. One person sees you as easy to work with, while another seems to bristle at your every word. It feels personal—but is it really about you?

Here's the liberating truth: most of the time, it's not.

The way people perceive and respond to you—especially early in a relationship—has far more to do with their world than with yours. Their reactions are filtered through past experiences, communication styles, personality traits and subconscious biases. In other words, you might be walking into a story that started long before you arrived.

Think about it: someone who's had a demanding boss may read your confidence as arrogance. Another person might see that same confidence as strong leadership. The behaviour hasn't changed—but their internal lens has. What they're responding to isn't your true self; it's a reflection of their own history and expectations.

Once a first impression forms, it tends to stick. Psychologists call this **confirmation bias**—the tendency to look for evidence that confirms what we already believe. If someone has decided you're difficult, they'll subconsciously hunt for proof, interpreting even neutral actions through that filter. On the flip side, if they've labelled you as capable or kind, they'll overlook your off days because it fits their existing picture of you.

That's why your experience with people isn't just shaped by who you are but by who they think you are. Their own stories and emotional baggage colour their openness, tone and willingness to collaborate.

Recognising this changes everything. Instead of internalising their reaction, you can take a breath and remember: *This might not be about me at all.* You don't have to shrink, defend or overcompensate. You can stay grounded in your values, speak with clarity and respond with calm. Over time, consistency and authenticity have a way of gently rewriting the narrative, helping others see you for who you truly are.

Making the Vibe Less Weird, More Workable

Now that we've wrapped our heads around this liberating truth—that someone else's reaction is rarely a personal review of you (and more like a preview of their inner movie)—you might be wondering, *Alright, but how do I make this awkward dynamic less ... awkward?*

Fair question.

Improving a tricky relationship isn't about turning into a people-whisperer overnight. It starts small—by noticing the exact moment you feel that inner jolt, the micro-trigger that comes from someone's tone, glance or comment. From there, it's about slowing down just enough to choose curiosity over assumption.

Step 1: Pause

Yes, actually pause. Take a breath (briefly—please, we're not aiming for fainting here). That moment of stillness stops you from launching into an internal courtroom drama where you're both judge and jury.

Step 2: Replay the moment with curiosity

Instead of mentally filing a complaint to HR in your head, try observing what happened as if you were watching security footage. *Hmm, their eyebrow twitched when I said, "Let's revisit that." Interesting.* Be playful with it. The goal isn't to diagnose them; it's to understand the subtle cues—tone, words, timing—that shaped the exchange.

Step 3: Spot the trigger

Now you're in detective mode. Look for surface-level clues: a pause that lasted too long, an unexpected sigh, an over-reaction, a sudden silence. Something in that moment probably brushed against one of their sensitivities or unmet expectations. Think of it as gathering data from the interaction—nothing more, nothing less.

Step 4: Discover their "why"

Once you've identified what triggered the response, it's time to explore why. What might be important to this person that caused that reaction? This is where you shift from detective to empathy wizard. Maybe they value precision, and your casual wording made them uneasy. Perhaps they care deeply about being heard, and your enthusiasm unintentionally drowned out their input. You're not reading their horoscope—you're simply tuning in to what matters to them.

In essence:

Step 3 = the event

Step 4 = the value behind it

By separating the "what" from the "why", you move from *What the heck just happened?* to *Ahh, that's what's important to them.* Once you know what someone values, you can work with them instead of around them—and that's the real power move in any relationship.

Try it in the next meeting: pause → replay → spot the trigger → guess the value → adjust one sentence you'd say differently next time.

Seeing Through a Cultural Lens

Throughout my corporate career, I've had the privilege of working with people from all over the world—and nothing has expanded my empathy more than that. Every culture brings its own rhythm, its own unspoken rules. What seems like distance or formality in one place may actually be a sign of respect in another. These experiences have taught me that adapting to someone else's values and communication style isn't just helpful—it's essential for meaningful collaboration.

One project in particular stands out. I was leading an initiative with stakeholders from Japan—a country that deeply values discipline, harmony and respect. One colleague had a very formal, structured style. His tone was measured, his facial expressions minimal, his feedback short and precise. At first, I wasn't sure how to read it. *Was he unhappy? Disengaged?* Having come from a more expressive culture, I had to fight the urge to overfill the silence.

Instead, I chose patience and consistency. I stayed open, friendly and professional. The project spanned several months, allowing us ample time to develop our understanding. Slowly, the dynamic began to change. He started sharing more thoughts, asking questions and, eventually, offering genuine collaboration. By the end, he became one of my strongest allies on future projects.

That experience taught me something lasting: *in some cultures, trust isn't handed out—it's earned through reliability and consistency.* Once that trust is built, it runs deep. It reminded me that effective cross-cultural collaboration isn't about changing who you are; it's about widening your lens and learning to see respect expressed in different forms.

Because, at its heart, **connection—whether across a desk, a culture or a difference of opinion—always begins with understanding what matters to the person on the other side.**

How to Move Forward When Your Effort to Connect Isn't Met Halfway

Have you ever heard the song "Fix You" by Coldplay? The first line—"When you try your best, but you don't succeed"—perfectly sums up a feeling most of us know too well. Especially when it comes to relationships.

Whether it's with a co-worker, a friend or a partner, there are moments when we put genuine effort into understanding the other person. We listen with curiosity, identify their values and try to build a bridge. We do everything "right". But sometimes, despite all that effort, we're met with resistance—or worse, things feel even more strained.

When that happens, it's natural to ask: *What now?*

If you've done your part and the connection still isn't working, it might be time to pause and reflect on whether the relationship is sustainable. Walking away isn't always an option—but you can always choose how much energy you continue to give. Protecting your wellbeing and emotional balance isn't selfish— it's responsible. ***Pouring your energy into a one-sided relationship leads to frustration, burnout and quiet resentment.***

That's where your CARE puzzle becomes your anchor. Before you decide what's next, check in with yourself:

Are my values still being respected?

Is this relationship helping me grow, or is it pulling me away from who I want to be?

You always have a choice, even if it's just about how you show up. Sometimes the healthiest thing you can do is step back, set clear boundaries and preserve your peace. The goal isn't always to fix the relationship—it's to stay in integrity with yourself.

Bringing It All Together: Key Takeaways

This chapter began with the idea of triggers—those unexpected emotional reactions that catch us off guard and leave us wondering why we feel so strongly. But, as we've explored, those reactions aren't random. Like Marty McFly in *Back to the Future*, whose fury was sparked by a simple word—"chicken"—our triggers reveal something more profound. They point to values or needs that are being challenged in the moment.

Your CARE puzzle—*comfort, ambition, renewal* and *equilibrium*—offers a way to decode those moments. It helps you understand how your values shape your emotions, your behaviour and your sense of fulfilment. When something in your environment clashes with those values, friction appears, and with it, the invitation to pause and reflect.

That's where *self-determination theory (SDT)* adds depth. It reminds us that we're all driven by three core needs: *autonomy (the freedom to choose), competence (the confidence to contribute)* and *relatedness (the feeling of connection)*. When these needs are unmet, emotional discomfort rises—and the triggers get louder.

Through personal stories of culture shock, reinvention and cross-cultural collaboration, we've seen that values aren't fixed—they evolve as life does. The real work isn't about holding on tightly to who you were but about staying connected to who you're becoming. Growth often feels uncomfortable, but that's how we build the kind of self-awareness that makes us both grounded and adaptable.

Because, ultimately, the friction, the awkwardness and even the relationships that didn't go as planned all have something to teach us. They're not detours; they're part of the process of becoming more aligned with who we truly are. Remember:

- Triggers aren't random—they signal a clash between external events and your internal values.

- Cultural awareness and life transitions can reshape values—this isn't loss but growth.

- Non-negotiable values define your boundaries—knowing and communicating them fosters healthier relationships.

- Asking "why" a reaction occurred is a powerful tool for self-awareness, boundary-setting and emotional resilience.

As you move forward, try to see each emotional reaction not as a setback but as a clue—a gentle nudge pointing you back to your values. The more you recognise what matters to you, the easier it becomes to navigate people, pressure, and change with clarity and calm. *Triggers lose their power when you meet them with curiosity instead of judgement.* And that's where the real growth begins: *not in avoiding discomfort but in learning from it, one honest pause at a time.*

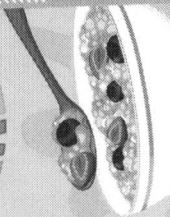

CEREAL

THE CHALLENGE

CONFUSION AND CLARITY

1) PAUSE
2) REPLAY
3) SPOT THE TRIGGER
4) DISCOVER WHY
5) ADJUST

ENGLISH TEACHER

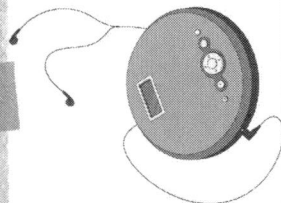

DICTIONARY

THE SOURCE

WHEN PEOPLE KNOW WHAT YOU STAND FOR, RELATIONSHIPS BECOME LESS ABOUT GUESSWORK AND MORE ABOUT GENUINE CONNECTION. AND THAT'S WHERE RESPECT, TRUST AND UNDERSTANDING TRULY BEGIN.

Fatima

Chapter Four

When The Mind Won't Let Go

There are times when my inner world feels suspiciously like the Star Wars universe—but not the fun kind with lightsabers and epic music. It's more like a chaotic town hall in my head. On one side is the light: my inner Jedi, calm and encouraging—"You're valuable." "You can create something beautiful." "This idea might work." On the other side is the dark: that uninvited voice that barges in with gloomy confidence—"Who do you think you are?" "Someone's done it better." "This is pointless." Somehow, even as the villain, it sounds convincing—like it's been stockpiling every awkward moment just so it can throw it at me when I'm trying to grow.

I've been caught in the middle more times than I can count. Some days, I try to reason with both sides. Other days, I stare at my to-do list, wondering how I went from hopeful to defeated in under five minutes. Lately, I just keep moving. Not because the dark voice disappears but because it doesn't get the final say. I nod at it—sometimes with a cheeky "thanks"—and carry on anyway.

If you've felt that tug-of-war—your own episode of The Force vs The Feels—you're not alone. Perhaps the real strength lies not in silencing the dark voice but in choosing to act while it's still speaking.

There's a Chinese philosophy, Yin and Yang, that reminds us that apparent opposites are interconnected. We all carry a two-for-one: the bright side we show the world—polite, composed, socially tidy—and the shadow we keep under wraps—sarcastic mutters, inconvenient feelings, the bits that don't always play nice. It's oddly freeing to admit we're not that innocent. Being human is dancing with both angel wings and all-too-human quirks.

Your inner Jedi and your inner Darth aren't enemies; they're two sides of one coin. The light brings clarity; the dark brings depth. Wholeness isn't perfection—it's making space for all of you and learning to move with both in balance. Balance isn't a destination; it's a practice. And you're already on that path.

Anxiety's Not the Enemy—It's Just a Really Loud Housemate

Some days, the inner debate is manageable. On others, the darker voice gains ground and everything feels heavier. Perhaps you've felt the chest-hollowness, a racing heart, pressure in your head, a ringing in your ears or the world turning strangely distant—like you're there but not really there. It's unsettling. Maybe you didn't know what it was until it had passed. Panic?

A meltdown? Or simply your mind waving a red flag that the inner balance is off?

When thoughts start to take over your body, the scramble to "get control back" can be frantic. Here's a reframe: one of the most powerful skills is recognising when anxiety stops helping and starts hijacking. Over time, you can develop a quiet internal switch—a checkpoint that says, "Hold on. This is too much." You're not trying to eliminate anxiety; you're putting it back in its place.

Anxiety isn't the villain. It's an emotion—like joy or sadness—that comes with a job. It can sharpen focus before a presentation or help you prepare for a tough conversation. That flutter? Sometimes it's fuel. But when anxiety sets up camp in every corner of your day with no real danger in sight, it becomes a noisy, freeloading housemate.

Would you let someone live rent-free, raid your fridge and keep you up with pointless chatter? *Exactly.* Don't evict anxiety forever—just retrain it. Show it to the guest room. Remind it who pays the emotional rent. Your mind is your home. You decide who stays, who visits and who gets five minutes on the porch.

House Rules: Anxiety Can Stay— But It Doesn't Get the Remote

Our inner strength steps in as a quiet but powerful ally—bringing structure to the chaos inside. Use the CARE puzzle as a practical compass to sort signal from noise. Not every thought is the truth. Not every feeling needs the floor. CARE gives us a meaningful check-in:

- **Comfort:** Do I feel safe and supported, or am I running on fear?

- **Ambition:** Is this thought driven by purpose or by pressure and self-doubt?

- **Renewal:** Have I rested and recharged, or am I powering through on empty?

- **Equilibrium:** Are work, relationships and health pulling me apart or moving in some kind of rhythm?

Say you're spiralling about not doing enough—your dark side whispers, "You're falling behind. Everyone's doing better." CARE steps in like a wise friend: "When did you last rest?" "Celebrate what you've done." "Are you chasing meaning or approval?" Then you remember: you're holding the remote. You don't have to keep the "Anxiety & Self-Doubt" channel on loop. You can switch to "Progress in Small Steps" or even "I'm Doing Fine, Actually".

Using CARE, we take back agency. We stop reacting and start responding—with more self-awareness, compassion and direction. It's not about eliminating anxiety; it's about changing our relationship with it—and remembering that, even in chaos, we still have choices.

I grew up in Caracas, Venezuela, where the weather is wonderfully predictable—warm, bright, tropical. The sun shows up like a dependable friend, and the temperature rarely strays far from a cosy 20–30°C (68–86°F). I fell in love with light, open skies and being outdoors. Later, in cities where winter stretches on and rain overstays its welcome, something shifted. The greyness didn't just fill the sky—it crept into my chest. On those cold, gloomy days, anxiety took the wheel. The rain wasn't just weather—it was a wall.

One day, mid-downpour and feeling caged, I snapped—in the best way. No umbrella, no plan. I pulled on my runners and left the house. I ran in the pouring rain for ten kilometres. Soaked, freezing, laughing like a kid breaking a rule on purpose. Somewhere between wet shoes and gasps for air, the anxiety cracked, and joy flooded in. I wasn't shrinking anymore. I was expanding. People stared; I didn't care. For the first time in days, I felt free.

That moment taught me something simple and powerful: freedom isn't only about circumstances—it's about choice. When life feels tight and heavy, sometimes the most healing thing you can do is surprise yourself. Step into discomfort. Laugh in the rain. Run when everything says "stay". You don't have to travel the world or solve every problem to regain balance. Sometimes all it takes is something a little wild, a little bold and deeply human to remember you're not just surviving the storm—you're dancing in it.

So here's my invitation: when your world feels small, your thoughts are too loud and the sky mirrors the fog within, do something that shakes your soul awake. Take an unexpected turn. Step outside the quiet rules you've built. Dare to feel again. It doesn't have to be a 10K run in the rain—maybe it's a spontaneous kitchen dance, a cold ocean dip or a walk with no destination. Whatever you choose, let it remind you that you're still here, still alive and still in charge of your story, even on the greyest days.

Let's Get Wet: Turning the Tides on Anxiety

I want to celebrate something beautifully simple: the power of cold water. It's one of the most grounding techniques I turn to when anxiety strikes. The instant shock of the cold helps calm racing thoughts and pulls me back into the present.

Cold-water immersion—whether a brisk shower, an ocean swim or a deliberate dip into chilly conditions—is increasingly recognised for its potential mental-health benefits. Emerging research suggests that brief cold exposure activates the sympathetic nervous system and can boost noradrenaline and beta-endorphins—chemicals linked to alertness, mood and pain modulation. This short, controlled stressor (hormesis) may train the body and mind to handle discomfort. Over time, regular cold exposure has been associated with reduced symptoms of anxiety and depression, possibly via improved vagus-nerve tone and a steadier stress response. It's not a cure-all or a substitute for medical care—so practise safely and check what's right for you.

One paper in *Medical Hypotheses* (Shevchuk, 2008) proposed that cold showers might help mood by stimulating the brain's "blue spot", a key source of noradrenaline. Studies of cold-water swimming in the UK have reported longer-term improvements in mental clarity, mood stability and general wellbeing. Again: complementary, not prescriptive.

One of my favourite winter memories is of the glassy, turquoise waters of Jervis Bay—a spot so beautiful and family-friendly that summer accommodation is scarce. So, we go in winter, when the crowds vanish and the bay feels like it's ours. On our last trip, a new ritual began. I zipped up my wetsuit, took a breath and ran straight into the icy water. It was electric. I screamed, laughed, splashed like a kid discovering the ocean for the first time. Beyond the joy and chaos, something deeper unfolded—my whole body dropped into stillness and clarity. The cold didn't shrink me—it woke me up.

From the shore, my husband and son watched, arms crossed, their faces wearing matching "no way" expressions. But curiosity is contagious. Minutes later, they were in—hesitant at first, then just as exhilarated. Before long, we were the unofficial entertainment for passing beachgoers, our laughter echoing across the sand. The next morning, some of those onlookers were in the water too, smiling and splashing in the same icy waves.

If you're feeling stuck or foggy, or you're craving something new, here's your invitation: come play in the cold. Let the chill strip away the noise and awaken something inside you. Let your inner child out for a swim. You might discover joy, connection and a rare kind of peace—the kind that arrives when you do something delightfully out of the ordinary.

Could Unrealistic Expectations Be Making Us Anxious?

Have you ever stopped to wonder what's really driving your anxiety? I've asked myself that many times—replaying moments, scanning my thoughts, searching for patterns. After plenty of reflection, a clearer picture emerged. My anxiety wasn't random—it was fuelled by two forces: one internal, one external. Together, they formed a loop.

A memory that still makes me laugh: I was twenty-five, about to get married and determined to look fabulous. The only issue? I wasn't in my "slimmest" phase. I decided to eat clean—except for one obstacle: Venezuelan food. If you know it, you know. We love our arepas—golden, warm corn patties of joy. Delicious? Absolutely. Diet-friendly? Not so much.

My boyfriend—now my husband—mentioned a friend

who'd lost weight in a single weekend. Friday to Monday. It sounded less like a diet and more like a miracle. I had to meet her.

Her "secret" was ... unconventional. Instead of smoothies or salads, she produced plaster—the kind used for broken arms—and wrapped my torso like I was auditioning for Mummy Bride 2000. Two hours later: a DIY plaster corset. The deal? Wear it all weekend, live on liquids and emerge on Monday transformed.

A few hours in, reality hit. I couldn't move properly. I was sweating, and the thought of sleeping trussed up like a piñata made me panic. The "diet" was basically sad juice and envy. In desperation, I begged, "Please, take this thing off me right now!" Scissors, freedom, relief. There was no miracle weight loss—but I did regain my liberty, which turned out to be the only weight I needed to lose.

That ridiculous experiment is a tidy metaphor for how far we go chasing unrealistic expectations. I believed a weekend wrapped like a mummy would fix my insecurities. It didn't—but it showed how easily we buy into extreme solutions to feel "enough".

Unrealistic expectations sneak in dressed as perfection, whispering that if we just try harder—or endure a little more—we'll finally measure up. The truth is different. We've all fallen down the rabbit hole of social media and glossy advertising: *Wear these jeans and you'll attract your soulmate. Sip this green juice and you'll look twenty again.* The message is clear: you're always one purchase away from being younger, cooler, richer, more lovable. Most of us end up with tighter jeans, an emptier wallet and juice that tastes like lawn clippings.

Then there's the friend—or, let's be honest, the frenemy—posting summit photos, arms outstretched like life itself is applauding. Meanwhile, my only big "trip" of late was to the supermarket, where I triumphed by remembering the reusable bags. At work, the stream of "So grateful to be part of the best team!" posts can make quiet wins—showing up, carrying the load, keeping life afloat—feel invisible. ***Perhaps the pressure comes less from our actions and more from our perceived responsibilities.***

Internal and external expectations can drive us mad if we let them define our worth. But what if the real wins aren't shiny at all? What if success is simply finding joy—and sharing it? Your kids are laughing at your terrible jokes. Your partner feels heard. Your pet is greeting you like you've returned from a year abroad instead of a brief trip to the letterbox.

A kind word that lifts someone's day. A moment of listening that helps a friend feel seen. These are the moments that matter: not perfection, but presence. Often, the most meaningful victories are already happening right in front of us.

When I first felt the pull to write this book, it came from a simple question: *what part of me is still searching for more?* I already had so much to be grateful for—a young family full of love and laughter, a career that challenged and shaped me, and a home in one of the most beautiful cities in the world. Yet a quiet space inside me asked to be understood.

It wasn't about wanting "more" in the material sense. It was about peeling back expectations, comparisons and the constant striving to find what was truly mine. Writing became my way of asking the questions I was too busy—or too afraid—to voice. On every page, I uncovered pieces of myself I hadn't heard in years.

Through this process, I saw how my own unrealistic expectations had been fuelling anxiety—and how small, grounded moments of presence brought me back to peace.

The book became more than words; it became a mirror—reflecting struggle and growth—and a path towards a kinder, more realistic version of myself.

I hope it does the same for you. As you read, pause—not with judgement, but with curiosity and kindness. You don't need to meet every external standard to live meaningfully. You can build a grounded, authentic version of yourself right where you are. *Sometimes, the most profound discoveries don't come from reaching higher but from looking closer at what's already within you.*

Bringing It All Together: Key Takeaways

This chapter blends story, philosophy and practice to reveal how inner and outer expectations fuel anxiety. It opens with the inner dialogue between the "light side" and the "dark side" of the mind—reminding us that doubt and encouragement coexist, much like Yin and Yang. Rather than silencing the darker voice, we acknowledge it, balance it and learn from it.

From there, the narrative shows how unrealistic expectations creep into daily life. The plaster-corset wedding story is a humorous but telling example of chasing extreme quick fixes only to end up more restricted than renewed. Add social media polish and workplace bragging, and external noise amplifies the impractical standards we place on ourselves. Anxiety often feeds not only on what others expect of us but on what we expect of ourselves.

The turning point is the CARE puzzle—comfort, ambition, renewal and equilibrium—a framework for calm and clarity when life feels out of balance. Paired with simple grounding practices like running in the rain or diving into cold water, CARE helps us see anxiety not as the enemy but as part of our humanity that can be understood, managed and softened with compassion.

Ultimately, the real victories aren't found in perfection but in presence—in quiet moments of kindness, laughter, connection and self-acceptance that bring us back to ourselves. By shifting from performance to authenticity, we rediscover freedom: the kind that comes from being fully human, flaws and all.

Quick fixes may tempt us, but real change grows from realistic, sustainable choices.

Chasing perfection can trap us; freedom comes from self-acceptance and balance.

Our funniest, most humbling failures often become our most powerful teachers.

SOMETIMES, THE MOST
PROFOUND DISCOVERIES
DON'T COME FROM
REACHING HIGHER, BUT
FROM LOOKING CLOSER
AT WHAT'S ALREADY
WITHIN YOU.

Fabina

MY WEDDING DAY

HESITATION BEFORE
THE COLD SPLASH

CHILLED OUT AFTER

Part Two

Ready to Trade "Stuck" for a Shot at Something New?

Part Two

Ready to Trade "Stuck" for a Shot at Something New?

If the first part helped you uncover the roots of self-doubt and the old scripts that kept you circling, this next part is about taking the brave step forward. It's about trading the comfort of being stuck for the possibility of something new—not by turning your life upside down overnight but by leaning into curiosity, loosening fear's grip and daring to ask different questions:

What if success simply meant living in a way that felt true to me?

What if my choices carried me closer to light, trust and purpose?

We start by rethinking what success really means—not the version you inherited from family, culture or society but the one that feels right for who you are now. Success in your twenties might have looked like freedom; later, it might look like resilience, connection or peace of mind. The point is, it changes as you do. This section invites you to redraw the map, experiment with small steps and take action without waiting for permission.

You'll also explore the role you play in every situation—how your choices, tone and energy shape the spaces around you. Are you the reason things move forward, or are you the reason they stall? These moments of awareness, whether in a meeting, at home or in your own self-talk, are where real influence begins. With the CARE check as your compass and a few simple tools for giving feedback that builds rather than blocks, you'll find what it means to be an enabler of progress—wherever you are.

Of course, momentum isn't always easy to keep. There will be times when the tunnel feels endless, when progress seems invisible. But even then, light finds its way in—sometimes as a flicker of kindness, sometimes as the courage to try again. The stories of people who have faced adversity with grace remind us that vision, courage and persistence can turn despair into progress. And when your own strength wavers, faith, community or connection can become the power that carries you forward.

Eventually, the journey brings you back to the one relationship you can't walk away from: the one with yourself. This is where you learn to face the questions you avoid, quiet the inner critic and practise the small shifts that build self-compassion. Because when you stop being your own obstacle and become your own ally, everything else—relationships, work and dreams—begins to align more naturally.

Taken together, these lessons form a bridge between awareness and action. They remind you that change rarely starts with giant leaps; it begins with the courage to move, even slightly, in a new direction. And once you trade "stuck" for even the smallest shot at something new, momentum has a way of multiplying.

So, are you ready? Let's start by redefining success—not by the world's rules but by your own. The next chapter is your first real step forward.

Chapter Five

What Does Success Look Like in Your Story?

Success isn't a one-size-fits-all journey. It's not everyone piling onto the same tour bus headed for the same destination. Real life is more like setting out on your own road trip: some people love the bright lights and fast pace, while others crave quiet landscapes and open skies. Success is like that—deeply personal, shaped by the turns you take, the stops you make and what you choose to notice along the way. What feels like a dream destination for me might not even appear on your map.

So, we're not chasing a checklist of what success should be. Instead, we're creating a route that fits you. For some, it's about achievement and momentum—the buzz of challenge and progress. For others, it's about balance and peace—the comfort of slower mornings and time for what truly matters. Neither is better; they're simply different expressions of fulfilment. Success isn't a single ticket everyone punches—it's the path you choose, step by step, aligned with what makes you feel most alive.

And here's the twist: I'm not just talking about this—I'm living it, too. Once again, I'm the guinea pig, figuring it out as I go. Think of this as a journey we're taking side by side. You're discovering what feels like your version of success while I share the stories, experiments and lessons from mine. The goal? To leave behind the pressure of doing life "right" and move towards a version of success that feels real, grounded and truly yours.

Bring your quirks, values and essence for the ride. Too often, we follow someone else's idea of success and end up feeling empty when we arrive. You might reach all the "right" milestones, but if they don't match who you are, they'll never feel like home. Success without your essence is just performing; success with your essence is living.

So here's the invitation: permit yourself to explore, to take detours and even to get a little lost. The best discoveries rarely happen on the straight path; instead, they show up in unexpected turns, quiet pauses and moments that catch you by surprise. Your path won't look like anyone else's—and that's precisely the point. When you trust yourself enough to wander, you don't just find success—you create it.

From Dreams to Reality:
How Our Vision of Success Grows With Us

My 20s: Belonging, Resilience, Opportunity

Success in my twenties wasn't planned—it was improvised. Every time I thought I'd "made it", life nudged me forward again. Back then, success looked carefree, fun and full of possibility. I was studying in Venezuela, living what I thought were my golden years. My friends and I formed a "study group", which often ended in laughter, music and dancing until sunrise. Success meant belonging and freedom.

But freedom can be fragile. Venezuela was at a turning point—big promises of prosperity soon turned to restrictions and uncertainty. Families, including mine, started feeling the walls close in. My idea of success shifted overnight—from carefree adventure to resilience, stability and holding onto hope when everything else felt unsteady. That's when I first understood that success isn't a fixed point—it adapts to what life demands from us.

Then came a turning point. One ordinary day at university, an Australian agency gave a talk about studying and working abroad. I sat there, captivated, as they described a place of opportunity, fairness and safety. It felt like someone had cracked open a window to a bigger, brighter world. That moment planted a seed of hope—and once it took root, there was no going back.

My 30s: Independence, Growth, Love

In 2001, I arrived in Australia—wide-eyed, nervous and completely unprepared. My first morning in our tiny apartment, sunlight spilled across the floor, and I thought: *Now what?* There was no script, no plan—just a blank page waiting to be written.

Back home, I'd been the diligent student while my mother and aunt ran the household. Suddenly, success meant something entirely different. It was about finding my feet—learning enough English to survive small talk, cooking without setting off the smoke alarm and mastering the washing machine without turning my clothes pink. Every small win became a personal celebration of independence.

Then came the challenge of finding a job. My first work experience? Receptionist. I was still translating half the conversation in my head while trying to sound confident. Day one was chaos—I hid in the bathroom more than once just to breathe. But little by little, the panic eased. What seemed impossible one week became manageable the next. A month later, I walked away with my first Australian reference and a newfound sense of capability. That small start opened the door to a whole new path in human resources, where I later specialised in the rewards field—a space that perfectly combined my love for people, numbers and meaningful progression.

A few years later, success shifted again—dramatically. After years of fertility treatments and heartbreak, I held my son for the first time. Every definition of success I'd carried until then dissolved in that instant. It wasn't about achievement anymore—it was about love, presence and purpose. Success became the quiet strength to keep showing up, even on the messy days.

If you're reading this in the middle of that season—whether as a parent, caregiver or someone juggling too many roles—you know. Success stops being about doing it all perfectly. It's about giving yourself grace as you continue to move forward.

Now: Choosing With Intention

Looking back, my life has unfolded in stages, each reshaping what success means. I left behind one world, built another, became a mother, and grew a career that allowed me to travel, connect and help design workplaces that recognise people as human beings, not just job titles.

But over time, I realised success isn't something you "arrive at" and hold forever—it evolves with you. That's why I started writing this book. It began as a pause to reflect, and it became a way to reconnect with what excites me. Writing became both a mirror and a compass—helping me see where I've been and where I'm heading next.

Redefining success isn't about chasing more. It's about aligning your choices with who you're becoming.

The Power of Seeing Before Becoming

Before any dream becomes reality, it has to be seen—not just with your eyes but with your imagination. Visualisation is that first spark: feeling, picturing and experiencing your dream as though it already exists.

When my husband and I were applying for our Australian visa back home, he became a master at the visa application process. Every time he went for a run, he carried a vivid image in his mind—seeing himself standing in Sydney, surrounded by new possibilities. He could picture the harbour, the Opera House, the skyline, even the feeling of arrival. His vision was so clear he could almost touch it.

Fast-forward to the day he finally did. The details weren't exactly as he'd imagined, but the dream had already done its work—it had pulled him forward. That was our lesson: visualisation doesn't just prepare your mind for the destination, it draws you towards it. Even if reality looks a little different, the act of seeing yourself there makes the journey feel inevitable.

So how does visualisation tie into my version of success? This book is the perfect example. Before a single word was written, I had to see it first—to picture what I wanted to share, how I tried to connect and why it mattered. I asked myself: *What would it take for this to feel possible?* That's when my own CARE puzzle came to life.

I imagined the comfort of creating a safe space for honest reflection, the ambition of turning my experiences into something meaningful, the renewal of pouring creativity back into myself through writing and the equilibrium of balancing personal stories with inspiring lessons.

Visualising the pieces helped me envision the finished book—not just as pages of words but as a mirror in which you, the reader, might recognise yourself. That vision kept me going. My goal wasn't simply to write a book but to build a genuine connection—one that encourages you to explore your own version of success.

What mattered most was staying true to myself—keeping my tone down-to-earth and honest, without pretending to have all the answers. I wanted this book to feel like a conversation, not a lecture. To get there, I embarked on an in-depth exploration. I devoured countless self-help books, paying attention not just to their words but to their tone, flow and design—the covers that caught my eye, the pages that made me pause. Each detail helped me notice what resonated and what didn't.

It was a long, sometimes messy process—years of trial and error, learning what felt authentic and what felt forced. I began as an amateur writer, trying to find my footing, but over time, I discovered a rhythm that felt unmistakably mine. And here's the truth: that style isn't about perfection.

It's about sharing what I've learnt in a way that feels human, relatable and (hopefully) inspiring for you too.

So here it is—how daydreaming became a storyboard and a storyboard became a book.

At one point, I sat at my laptop and created a simple visual map. Nothing fancy—just a collection of images that brought my dream to life and helped me see my CARE puzzle take shape.

- **Comfort:** A writer by a window, coffee mug in hand, ideas flowing freely—a reminder that I needed a safe and inspiring space to create.

- **Ambition:** A woman signing her book in a busy bookstore—the belief that this dream could one day reach others.

- **Renewal:** My "editor-in-chief", Teddy, curled up beside me—proof that joy and rest fuel creativity.

- **Equilibrium:** A photo of my family laughing together—a reminder that chasing a dream doesn't have to mean losing balance.

That storyboard became more than pretty pictures—it became my personal map to success. And here's my invitation to you: create your own CARE puzzle storyboard. Gather images that reflect your comfort, ambition, renewal and equilibrium, and let them guide you towards the version of success that feels right for you.

Try it once with a dream or project you care about, and you'll see how much clearer the path becomes. ***Be brave, trust yourself, and take the first step—your dream is already in your hands, waiting for you to make it real.***

Daydreaming Storyboard

Equilibrium

Ambition

Comfort

Renewal

The Power of Small Experiments

Let's imagine your dream of success is to become a musician. The only catch? You're in your forties, and you've never had a single music lesson in your life. Still, whenever you're home alone, you crank up your favourite Guns N' Roses track, grab the nearest broom and—just like that—it becomes your electric guitar. Suddenly, you're not just a fan; you're the headliner of your own living room concert. Not one song, not two—you've got a full four-track setlist, belting it out like Axl Rose himself while nailing every invisible guitar solo.

Now, maybe you don't dream of touring the world, but deep down you've always had that playful urge to learn the guitar—just enough to jam with friends, play for your family or sneak in a few songs at a local pub. And that's the point: *success doesn't have to mean "all or nothing"*. Sometimes it's about turning that private concert into a small, joyful reality that brings you—and maybe a few lucky listeners—a whole lot of fun.

Or your dream is to step onto a stage, not just as a financial planner but as a confident speaker who makes money conversations less intimidating. You've got years of experience behind you, and you can already picture yourself transforming that knowledge into courses designed for people who've never quite felt "money savvy". Imagine the impact—you're not just teaching finance, you're giving people the confidence to see money as a tool for freedom, not a source of stress.

Whatever your small project looks like, its real power is that it becomes the stepping stone to something uniquely yours—a contribution only you can make to the world. You don't need anyone's permission to begin. The moment you give your idea shape, your life expands; you've already elevated your life experience. And here's the magic: *once your project has a body and a heartbeat, it not only changes you—it can inspire and uplift others, too.*

When it came to this book, I knew no one else was going to make it happen for me. As a first-time self-publisher, the process was equal parts daunting and thrilling. I had no professional background in publishing, yet step by step, I built a path that turned a dream into something tangible. Here's what that looked like.

Step 1: Clarify the vision

I had to define what I wanted to say, who I wanted to reach and how I wanted the book to feel. Without a clear vision, I knew I'd go in circles.

Step 2: Build a writing rhythm

I carved out regular writing time and captured every spark of inspiration—on my phone, in photos or scribbled on notes. Those fragments became the foundation of my chapters.

Step 3: Write—and rewrite

The manuscript didn't arrive in one sweep—it was drafted, reshaped and refined. Each rewrite made it clearer, stronger and closer to what I imagined.

Step 4: Learn the world of self-publishing

This was a whole education in itself. I had to:

- understand the legal responsibilities of being an author in Australia, including copyright

- explore literature related to the book topics and weave in my own experiences

- experiment with DIY editing, design, formatting and metadata

- research printing, publishing and simple marketing strategies.

Was it overwhelming? Absolutely. But more than that, it was energising. Every challenge stretched me beyond what I thought I was capable of. By permitting myself to explore something different, I also allowed myself to evolve. Some people might see a project like this as intimidating, but for me, it was an opportunity to do something new—*a reminder that success often lives not in certainty but in the courage to begin.*

Your version of success will look completely different from mine—and that's precisely how it should be. To help you kickstart your own journey, I've included a simple chart that you can use. Think of it as your launchpad, your "why not start today?" moment. Dive in, play with it and make it yours.

Intention

Define the what, who and how.

1

Book Time for Action

Make your project be part of your schedule.

2

Work on it

Start and review your project, make sure that you are happy with what you are creating

3

Self-Learning

Familiarise yourself with your project constantly, read relevant literature, and learn to leverage technology effectively.

4

Produce Outcome

Transform your vision or project into a vibrant reality!

5

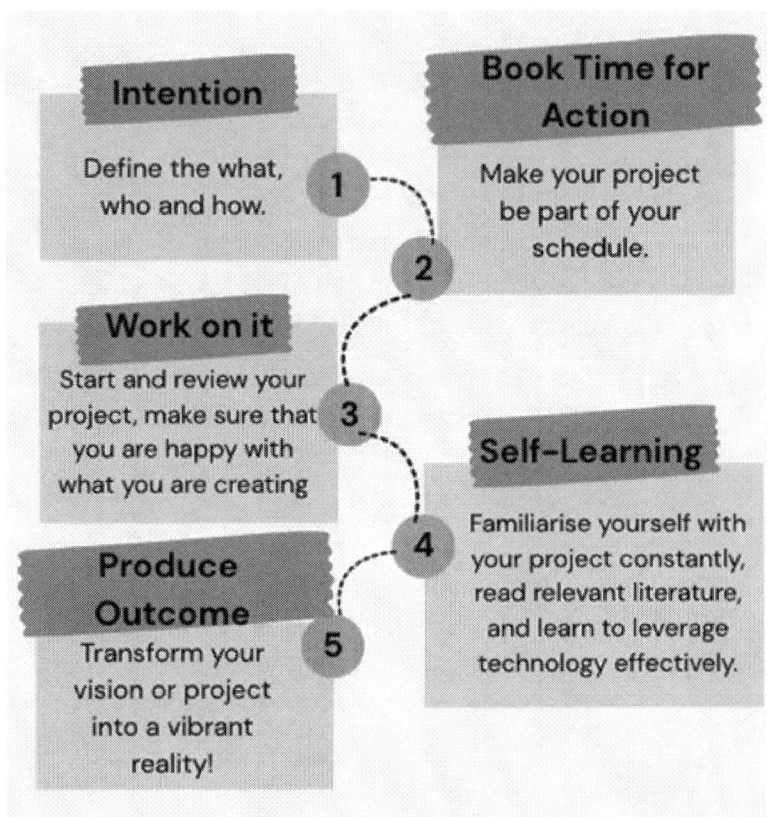

Success vs. Paralysis: How to Get Unstuck and Move Forward

Remember that childhood game where the music plays, everyone dances and then—*bam*—it stops and you have to freeze like a statue? That's life, sometimes. One moment you're moving forward with energy, and the next you're frozen—unsure if you should take another step, waiting for someone else to give you the green light.

I've had plenty of those moments. Some days, I feel

unstoppable—ideas flow, energy is high and I'm ready to take on the world. On other days, doubts creep in and I find myself hesitating, questioning whether what I'm creating truly matters. It's not about being incapable—it's that self-doubt has a sneaky way of pressing pause on our progress. The trick is remembering that, just like in the game, you don't actually need permission to start moving again.

What holds us back isn't usually a lack of talent—it's the fear of what others might think or the worry that we're not ready. Sometimes it's simply not knowing where to begin, so the first step feels impossible. That hesitation can be paralysing, but it doesn't have to be.

Here's the truth: most people are too focused on their own lives to scrutinise ours as closely as we think. The harsh critic we imagine "out there" is often just our inner voice turned up too loud. And even when others do have opinions, they fade quickly. What lingers is the regret of not trying.

No one starts as an expert. Every person you admire had a messy, awkward beginning. Skill comes from practice, not perfection at the starting line.

So, when you're not sure where to start—start small. Break your dream down into the tiniest steps and tackle them one at a time. Each action, however small, proves that you're capable of moving forward. Progress doesn't belong to the most confident; it belongs to the ones willing to begin.

Whenever I feel stuck, I hit my personal reset button—I employ a few simple habits that help me rewind, recharge and jump back in with fresh energy.

Step 1: Start ridiculously small

Big goals can feel paralysing because we focus on the mountain instead of taking the first step. Shrink it down. If your dream is to write a book, start with one messy paragraph—or one sentence. If your goal is fitness, don't aim for a two-hour session; take a ten-minute walk. Action, however small, melts the freeze.

Example: When I was stuck on a chapter, I told myself, "just write one line you'd text a friend". That line turned into a page.

Step 2: Change your environment

Sometimes we're not stuck because we lack ability but because our surroundings keep us stagnant. A new setting can shift your mindset. Work from a café, sit in a park or simply clear your desk. A fresh space reminds your brain that something new is possible.

Example: I once took my laptop to the library after feeling blocked at home. The change of scenery sparked focus, and the ideas started flowing again.

Step 3: Borrow energy from others

When we feel stuck, we tend to isolate—but connection creates momentum. Share your idea with a supportive friend, join a group or watch someone else doing what you aspire to do. Energy is contagious.

Example: I joined a local writing circle—simply to listen and learn. Hearing others read reignited my motivation to write.

So many brilliant ideas never see the light because of fear.

Fear of criticism is a thief—it steals your chance to create something meaningful before it's even begun. *The truth is, people will always have opinions, but they don't pay the price for your regrets—you do.*

That's why it's so important to give your dreams a chance to live. Imagine the difference between an idea you never dared to share and one that grows into something real. Your job isn't to please everyone; it's to honour what's inside you. Be bold enough to take that step, even if your voice shakes. In the end, it's better to be judged for trying than to silence yourself and wonder forever, *What if?*

Bringing It All Together: Key Takeaways

This chapter has been about redefining success—shifting it away from society's checklists and towards a more personal, evolving journey. Through my story—from Venezuela to Australia, from carefree student days to motherhood and professional growth—I've shown how success changes shape with every season of life. It isn't one-size-fits-all, and it certainly isn't static.

Success isn't about ticking off someone else's "top 10 list". It's about creating a map that reflects your values, your quirks and your essence. Whether through small experiments, visualising the next step or daring to begin even when fear whispers you can't, success becomes possible when you honour what feels real to you. It doesn't grow from perfection or permission—it grows from action, resilience and the courage to keep showing up.

So, as you close this chapter, keep these three reminders close—not as rules but as gentle truths for the road ahead:

- Regret weighs more than criticism. Opinions fade, but the sting of never trying lingers longer.

- Momentum beats confidence. You don't need to feel ready—just start. Confidence grows through motion.

- Your path is your gift. The detours and wrong turns aren't distractions; they're the very things that make your version of success worth living.

EMBARKING ON MY FIRST JOB

GRADUATION DAY

NOW CHOOSING WITH INTENTION

MOTHERHOOD

REDEFINING SUCCESS
ISN'T ABOUT CHOOSING
MORE. IT'S ABOUT
ALIGNING YOUR CHOICES
WITH WHO YOU'RE
BECOMING.

Fatima

Chapter Six

Be the Reason It Works, Not Why It Breaks

Life keeps showing me that it's not the big moves that make things work; it's shaped by the small choices we make, moment to moment. In a family decision, a group project or a high-stakes meeting, one person can say, "This will never work," and shut everything down, or lean in with, "What if we try it this way?" That single choice flips the energy from frustration to problem-solving.

Choosing to be the reason something works by listening, adapting and supporting shapes outcomes and the experience people have along the way.

I've seen the flip side, too, in myself and in others. Without meaning to, we sometimes become the reason things break—insisting on being right, withholding help because "it's not my problem" or letting ego lead. Progress doesn't require perfect answers; it asks for presence, accountability and generosity. If you keep choosing to show up that way—in your job and your life—you become the one people turn to when it matters most.

For leaders, this is non-negotiable. Leadership isn't just task direction; it's creating an environment where people can succeed. Fear shuts ideas down; curiosity and clarity invite them in. Leaders who say, "Bring me challenges, and we'll find the solution together," spark ownership and collaboration. Leaders who are vague, punitive or risk-averse breed silence and second-guessing. Choosing to be the reason it works is what separates leaders who leave a legacy from those who leave frustration.

This truth also applies at home. Parents who model resilience and accountability teach that obstacles are part of the journey. Young people who adopt this mindset early unlock doors. They ask, "How can I help?" and take responsibility for their next step. In every role—leader, parent, student—we either break momentum or build it.

You know I love a story that nudges reflection. Here's a true one.

He was a boy who spoke so late that some people thought there was something wrong with him. He questioned authority instead of memorising answers and was labelled lazy. He failed his first university entrance exam. When he finally graduated, professors refused to recommend him for academic posts. He took a job in a patent office—hardly the picture of a rising star. From the outside, he appeared to be destined for mediocrity.

Yet, in that obscurity, without the weight of approval, his mind opened new worlds. He reframed time, space and energy. The very qualities mocked in him—independence, relentless questioning—fuelled the breakthroughs that changed science. The "failure" was Albert Einstein. **His story is a reminder: rejection can be a doorway, and what others dismiss in you may be your advantage.**

What qualities in you—once doubted—might be the keys to your most significant success?

Success is rarely built in isolation. It's shaped by how we step into our roles and the responsibility we're willing to carry. Setbacks reveal strengths; choices reveal character. Embrace accountability and purpose, and watch challenges turn into opportunities for impact.

Let's look at how this plays out in each role.

Our Roles and Responsibilities

This next section is about the hats we wear and the ripple effect of how we wear them. Whether you're parenting, leading a team, navigating friendships or simply trying to be a good human, your choices either create momentum or stall it. Roles aren't job titles or family labels; they're living spaces where your values meet real life. And *responsibility isn't punishment—it's the privilege of shaping what happens next.*

You'll notice a theme running through these pages: presence over perfection. When we show up with clarity, curiosity and care, we become enablers—people who make things work. When we show up rushed, triggered or checked out, we drift into blocking—shutting ideas down, confusing expectations or shrinking someone else's courage. Neither identity is fixed. With a slight shift in language, boundaries or energy, we can change the temperature of a room and the trajectory of a day.

Think of what follows as a set of gentle spotlights, each aimed at a different role: parent, youth, leader, peer and, finally, *you*. Each message offers perspective, a few practical handles and an invitation to act. As you read, try this: *choose one role you hold most often and one tiny behaviour to adjust— something you can do within the next 48 hours.* Ask a better question. Clarify a "why". Offer specifics instead of vague critique. Protect a boundary without hardening your heart.

If you want a compass while you read, keep your inner CARE puzzle close and notice which piece is strong, which one needs attention and how that alignment shifts you from blocking to enabling. This is where growth becomes visible: not in big declarations but in small, repeatable choices that turn roles into relationships and responsibility into impact.

Message to Parents

As a parent, I've come to realise how easily we repeat the patterns we grew up with, often without meaning to. Kids don't arrive with an instruction manual, and most of us are just doing our best with the knowledge and tools we have. But parenting isn't only about providing care; it's also about checking in with ourselves and asking how deeply we're truly connecting with our children. The best measure of parenting isn't perfection— it's presence. It's our willingness to listen with curiosity, to step into our children's world without judgement, and to give them the freedom to be who they are.

I'll be honest—this isn't always easy. It's frustrating to watch your child make choices that could be smoother with your guidance. Yet we have to remember: we won't be here forever. The sooner children have the chance to explore, stumble and succeed on their own, the better equipped they'll be to carve their path and define success on their own terms.

One of the most brutal truths for parents to face is asking ourselves why we respond the way we do. *Are we truly guiding them, or are we protecting our own ego?* Sometimes, when a child pushes back, we react out of pride or frustration, seeking control rather than offering guidance. Other times, we confuse discipline with domination, thinking we're teaching when we're actually silencing. The real challenge—and opportunity—is to choose actions that foster safety rather than fear, curiosity rather than shame. When we parent from guidance instead of ego, we create a home where our children feel secure enough to grow, explore and come back to us—not because they must but because they want to.

When grief first entered my life after my mum passed away, I was flooded by emotions I didn't know how to carry. Grief has its stages—denial, anger, bargaining, depression and, eventually, acceptance—and while for some it takes years, for me it took two. Those first six months were the hardest. I was restless, short-tempered and distracted. My young son felt it most. The patience and warmth he once knew had faded. My grief had quietly reshaped me into someone I hardly recognised.

Then came the moment that cracked me open. One afternoon, as I hurried him out of the car, frustration spilled over. He was only six, but his gentle question cut through all the noise: "Why are you so different now? I miss you the way you used to be." His words stopped me cold. I realised how my sadness had started to spill over onto him. The next day, I sought professional help. Healing wasn't instant, but over time, trust returned—and with it, his smile.

That experience taught me something I'll carry forever: ***being a parent doesn't mean our children should absorb our pain.*** Even in our hardest seasons, they deserve our love, patience and a safe place to simply be children.

Message to the Youth

You are living in the most powerful chapter of your life: your youth. This is the season where curiosity is your compass and mistakes are not failures but adventures in disguise. Think of life right now like an open-world video game: every choice unlocks a new level, every challenge adds experience, and yes, sometimes you'll lose a life, but you always get to respawn with more wisdom. Don't be afraid of standing out, asking bold questions or dreaming bigger than the world tells you is possible. The spark you carry right now is meant to light the way, not just for you but for others who will follow.

Youth is about creating momentum. If you want to change, start making the change. To lead effectively, take the initiative. If you're going to build something that lasts, begin today, even if it feels small. Imagine your energy as unlimited Wi-Fi. Connect it to bold ideas, new people and wild dreams. But as you do, never forget that real strength comes with respect and consideration. ***The world doesn't just need fearless voices—it needs voices that know how to listen, how to uplift and how to recognise the dignity in others. It's easy to be loud, but it's far more powerful to be kind while being bold.***

And remember: joy is as important as ambition. Laugh loudly, dance like it's TikTok—even if no one hits "like"— and celebrate the small victories as if they were Oscars. You don't need to have everything figured out to live fully in the present. *Youth is your playground, your laboratory, your stage, so don't just exist in it—perform in it.* Chase the experiences that make your heart race, invest in friendships that lift you higher and believe in yourself with a stubborn kind of joy. Because one day, when you look back, you'll see that youth wasn't just the beginning—it was the fire that fuelled everything after.

When I decided to pack my bags and move to Australia, most people back home had no idea what my country was about to undergo. Migration wasn't exactly a popular idea back then, and let's just say it didn't win me any popularity contests. I had mates who would look me straight in the eye and call me a "sellout"—as if boarding a plane was the same as betraying the motherland. Yeah, it stung at first. Nobody likes being branded a traitor just for chasing a different postcode.

But here's the thing: sometimes being called a sellout just means you've cashed in on the better deal. And honestly? That move turned out to be the best investment of my life. Sure, I traded late-night banter with my old crew for the sound of kookaburras laughing at dawn, and I swapped arepas for meat pies. But I also gained new horizons, new friends and a country that taught me resilience through dodging magpies during spring. Most importantly, I learnt that choices matter most when they're rooted in respect—for yourself, for others and for the world you're shaping. Looking back, they called it selling out, but I was buying into a life I wouldn't trade for anything.

Message to Leaders

Before you dive into charts, spreadsheets and endless KPIs, pause for a moment and remember this: you don't lead numbers—you lead people. Each person who reports to you is more than just a position or a line in a budget. They're a whole human being with stories, ideas, fears and potential waiting to be unlocked.

Your leadership is like the weather—it sets the climate for everyone around you. Sunshine leadership brings warmth, clarity and growth. Storm-cloud leadership leaves people walking on eggshells, bracing for the next downpour. The tone you set ripples far beyond your immediate team; it shapes trust, creativity and culture. Every conversation, email or meeting is a choice: will you be the kind of leader who fuels progress, or will you be the type that people quietly wish they could mute on Zoom?

Authentic leadership is more than decision-making; it's energy-making. Enablers recognise that their presence either expands or constricts others. They ask, *What energy do I bring into this room?* and *What happens to others when I speak?* A leader who enables growth doesn't need all the answers. Instead, they create the conditions where answers can surface. They make space for quieter voices, half-formed ideas and human emotions. They understand that leadership is less about control and more about clarity.

Blocker leaders, on the other hand, may not even realise they're blocking. It happens in subtle ways—interrupting instead of listening, dismissing ideas that feel risky or using fear disguised as "high standards". They often measure success by output but overlook the input that truly matters: trust. Over time, their teams shrink in headcount and in spirit. Innovation fades, initiative stalls. People tend to do just enough to stay safe.

So here's a challenge for any leader brave enough to pause:

- When did you last listen without planning your response?

- Do people feel free to speak, or do they filter themselves first?

- After meeting with you, do they leave energised or deflated?

These questions aren't about guilt; they're about awareness. Because awareness is what separates good managers from great leaders. Once you notice your patterns, you can change them. You can turn criticism into curiosity, replace command with collaboration and move from compliance to commitment.

Enabling leadership isn't soft—it's smart. It builds accountability through trust, not fear. It turns mistakes into learning moments and feedback into forward motion. And it begins with a single decision that echoes through every corner of your team: *Will I be the reason this works or the reason it breaks?*

Message to Peers

We're in this together, shoulder to shoulder. Teams aren't meant to be arenas of constant comparison, where one person's win feels like another's loss. They're more like a band: if the drummer misses a beat, the whole song stumbles; if the guitarist hogs the solo, the magic fades. Being supportive doesn't mean always agreeing; it means tuning in, playing in harmony and keeping the bigger picture in focus. After all, wouldn't you rather work with a crew that cheers each other on than one quietly counting how many notes you've missed?

When leaders see people, not numbers, and peers lift each

other rather than compete for air, the workplace transforms. It stops feeling like a battlefield and starts feeling like a well-run kitchen: everyone knows their role, respects each other's craft, and together they create something far greater than the sum of its parts. That's the kind of culture where people feel safe to try, respected enough to stay and motivated to give their best without fear of being cut down. Because *at the end of the day, numbers don't make people succeed—people make numbers succeed.*

Throughout my career, I've had the pleasure of working with brilliant professionals from whom I've learnt a great deal—and I've learnt just as much from the more difficult ones. Every person and every situation has something to teach us. What truly matters isn't just what we encounter but how we weave those lessons into how we show up—for our direct reports, for our peers and for ourselves.

That's where the real responsibility lies: *in recognising that we're not passengers of workplace culture; we're drivers of it.* Yes, organisations face pressure and must evolve fast to stay relevant, but speed and stress don't permit us to drop respect or decency at the door. Every interaction, every decision, every word spoken is a choice—one that can either weaken trust or strengthen it, divide or unite.

The results we see in our teams and projects aren't abstract outcomes floating above us—they're the sum of our daily choices. And here's the reflection: *You are part of that sum. You can choose to add value or subtract from it, thereby fuelling growth or draining it. The power to shape culture isn't "out there" somewhere in senior management—it's right here, in our hands.*

Message to YOU, the Reader

You're here for a reason. Maybe you picked up this book out of curiosity, like peeking into the fridge at midnight, hoping to find something you didn't even know you were craving. Or maybe you're here because you can feel a shift coming: that quiet nudge inside whispering, *it's time*. Whatever brought you here, it wasn't by chance. Every page you turn is a step on a hiking trail—sometimes smooth, sometimes steep, but always guiding you closer to the person you're becoming.

This book isn't a GPS with a perfect route, nor a manual of dull, step-by-step instructions. Think of it more like a backpack, packed with snacks and maps from those who've walked the path before you. Along the way, you'll stumble upon ideas that make you laugh, stories that sting like a papercut and reflections that land as softly as a reminder from a friend. Growth is messy, unpredictable and sometimes downright funny, like trying to pitch a tent in the wind. But it's in the fumbling that you figure out who you really are.

By the time you reach the last page, I hope you'll see your journey like a playlist: some songs make you dance, others make you cry, but together they tell your story. This book can offer beats, lyrics and rhythm—but the real music? That's yours to sing.

So read with curiosity. Laugh at the awkward bits. Take what resonates and make it your own. Because if you're holding this book right now, you've already proved one thing: you're ready for the ride.

Become an Enabler, Not a Blocker

So here we are, standing at the crossroads of possibility. On one side stands the enabler—that wise, supportive version of you who says, "Yes, let's do this—I'll even bring snacks." On the other hand, the shadow of the blocker—the part of you that folds its arms, raises an eyebrow and mutters, "Really? You thought that was a good idea?"

The truth is, we all carry both within us. Sometimes it's clear which one is steering the ship; you can feel yourself breathing life into an idea, fuelling momentum or cheering on a fresh start. Other times, it's murkier. Confusion creeping in like an uninvited guest at a dinner party: *Was it my hesitation that stalled things, or was it someone else's tangle that threw me off course?*

And here comes the million-dollar question: how do you know if you're genuinely helping ... or quietly making things more complicated than they need to be?

Here is where your inner CARE puzzle becomes your compass, a guide made of four pieces: comfort, ambition, renewal and equilibrium. When these align, clarity flows. When they scatter, nothing quite fits, and even good intentions can end up blocking progress. The good news? When you know how to use CARE, you can identify the role you're playing: enabler, blocker or someone who needs a break before making another decision.

Let's pause here.

Before rushing to label yourself, ask: *Where am I standing within my CARE puzzle?*

Each piece acts like a compass point. Together, they reveal not just who you are but how you show up when ideas, projects or opportunities land at your door.

Step 1: Comfort (C)—your grounding place

Ask yourself:

- Am I safe, centred and calm enough to respond thoughtfully?

- Or am I tense, defensive or uneasy right now?

Quick check: When your actions come from fear or discomfort, you're likely to block. When they arise from a state of grounded calm, you enable clarity and connection.

Step 2: Ambition (A)—your mark on the world

Ask yourself:

- Does this idea or project align with values and a purpose?

- Am I reacting because it threatens my ego or because it genuinely doesn't fit the bigger picture I want to build?

Quick check: When your response aligns with purpose, you enable progress. When it's rooted in competition or resistance to growth, you're blocking.

Step 3: Renewal (R)—your energy and strength

Ask yourself:

- Do I have the energy and focus to make a positive contribution?

- Or am I running on empty, saying "no" simply because I'm exhausted?

Quick check: A "no" from depletion is a blockage disguised as self-protection. A "yes" or even a "not now, but soon" offered from renewed energy enables.

Step 4: Equilibrium (E)—your emotional balance

Ask yourself:

- Am I emotionally balanced, or are my triggers clouding my judgement?
- Can I separate what I feel from what's best for the situation?

Quick check: If your emotions spill over and blur the issue, you may be blocking. When you respond with calm discernment, you're enabling.

Pulling It Together—The CARE Check

Whenever you're unsure, take a moment for a quick CARE check:

C—Comfort: Am I grounded?

A—Ambition: Am I aligned with purpose?

R—Renewal: Am I energised?

E—Equilibrium: Am I emotionally balanced?

If most of your answers lean towards "yes", you're probably enabling growth. If you find more "noes", you might be blocking, not out of evil intent but because something inside your CARE puzzle is out of alignment.

Closing Reflection

The next time confusion creeps in and you wonder whether you're helping or hindering, let your CARE puzzle serve as a mirror. Ask each piece to speak, and its answers will tell you whether you're standing as an enabler who opens doors or as a blocker who, knowingly or not, closes them.

And once you see it clearly, don't stop at awareness. Act on it. If you're an enabler, wonderful—keep the momentum rolling, add fuel to the fire and yes, bring cake to the meeting. But if you catch yourself blocking, congratulations, you've just spotted growth in action. Now the question becomes: *Will you double down and guard the gate like a dragon, or will you shift, adjust and let a good idea through?* Awareness is only half the battle. The real power lies in what you choose to do once the mirror shows you who you are.

Constructive vs Unhelpful Input

We've all had "helpful" advice that lands like a manual missing half the pages. Feedback says as much about the giver as the receiver. People speak from their lens, history, biases and even breakfast.

The goal isn't dodging feedback; it's decoding it. Ask: *Is this about me or about them?* If it's their baggage, smile and slide the suitcase back. If it sheds light, take the gift, even if it's clumsily wrapped.

Input With Benefits (The Enabler's Version)

Enablers are specific, action-based and respectful.

Not "do better" but "your ideas are strong—slow down in the middle so your message really lands". They focus on behaviours and outcomes, protect dignity and reconnect you to your "why".

How to use it:

- Listen for clarity and examples.

- Check tone and intention. Do you feel encouraged and challenged, not judged?

- Ask: "Could you give an example?" "What would improvement look like?"

When Advice Feels Like a Brick Wall (the Blocker's Edition)

Blocker feedback is vague, negative or biased: "This will never work." "You're not good at that." It shuts things down.

How to handle it:

- Separate emotion from information; look for any usable clue.

- Ask, "What specifically makes you think that?" If they can't answer, it's their lens.

- Don't internalise the sting. Recycle what helps; bin the rest.

And when giving input, check your approach: are you leaving gentle fingerprints—or muddy bootprints?

When Words Leave a Mark

Our feedback is never just ours; it becomes part of someone else's story. If we're clear, kind and constructive, we're the friend who hands over a map (and maybe a snack) for the journey. But if we're vague, dismissive or laced with personal bias, we might as well be handing them a broken compass and a lecture on why they're lost.

So here's the challenge: reflect on your style. Do you want to be remembered as the voice that unlocked doors or the one that accidentally slammed them shut while everyone else was still in the hallway?

Funny thing about advice: sometimes the crummiest lines end up being the most powerful. At the time, they sound like the kind of "wisdom" you'd find scribbled on a bathroom wall—not exactly life-changing material. But life has this sneaky way of marinating bad advice until it suddenly tastes like something worth keeping.

Take my Auntie Tica. One day, as she sat in her wheelchair on the balcony of my family home in Caracas, she looked at me and said, "Darling, the trick to a happy life is simple— don't expect much, that way you'll never be disappointed."

At first, I thought, *Wow, thanks, Tica. So, the grand secret is to aim low and applaud yourself when you trip over nothing?* Not exactly the motivational pep talk I was hoping for.

But here's the twist—hidden beneath her blunt delivery was a quiet gem. What Tica was really pointing to (without the sugar-coating) was the weight of expectations. The tighter you grip a specific result, the more you strangle joy and creativity out of the process. When I flipped her advice on its head, it became one of the best lessons I've ever learnt: set your intention, give it your best, but don't anchor your happiness to the outcome.

Tica wasn't telling me to settle. She was teaching me to *breathe*. To let go a little. To leave space for life's surprises to show up.

And if she were here to add her classic punchline, she'd probably grin and say, "Besides, darling, low expectations make every success feel like winning the lottery—now go buy yourself a ticket!"

Bringing It All Together: Key Takeaways

This chapter explores a powerful truth: our everyday choices—big or small—determine whether we act as enablers (those who make things work) or blockers (those who stand in the way). From classrooms and family projects to boardrooms and high-stakes meetings, the way we show up can shift an entire outcome. A single "what if?" offered in the middle of a stuck conversation can reignite progress, just as a quick "this will never work" can quietly deflate it. *Whether we're leaders, parents, peers or simply individuals navigating daily life, the responsibility is the same: to lead with accountability, respect and presence— not ego or indifference.*

Feedback plays a central role in life. Constructive input from an enabler is clear, actionable and encouraging. Blocker feedback, on the other hand, is vague, critical and deflating. *The challenge for all of us is to notice which style we use and choose words that open doors rather than close them.* Every interaction leaves a trace.

The chapter lands on a profoundly human note: when we loosen our grip on outcomes, we make room for growth—and for life to delight us in ways we couldn't have planned.

Woven through reflections on youth, leadership, migration and grief, one message stands out: *we all hold the power to create momentum or halt it.* The way we show up—in words, energy and intent—shapes not only our own path but the stories of those who walk beside us.

THE WORLD DOESN'T JUST NEED FEARLESS VOICES—IT NEEDS VOICES THAT KNOW HOW TO LISTEN, HOW TO UPLIFT AND HOW TO RECOGNISE THE DIGNITY IN OTHERS. IT'S EASY TO BE LOUD, BUT IT'S FAR MORE POWERFUL TO BE KIND WHILE BEING BOLD.

Fatima

THE NEXT GENERATION

BE AN ENABLER

ADD VALUE TOGETHER

GENERATIONAL COLLABORATION

Chapter Seven
Finding Light When the Tunnel Feels Endless

The tunnel, in life, is that stretch between endings and beginnings—the uncertain space where what once made sense no longer fits and what comes next hasn't yet revealed itself. It's the quiet in-between where clarity fades, routines lose meaning and progress feels invisible. You start to wonder if the light you're walking towards even exists, or if you've been chasing an illusion.

I remember feeling this way when I left my home country and arrived in Australia. Everything was new—the rhythm of the language, the faces, even the quiet ache of missing what I'd left behind. I carried doubts heavier than my suitcase: Would I belong? Would the sacrifice be worth it? For a while, I couldn't see the light at all.

Slowly, though, small shards of light appeared. A stranger's smile as they helped me on a bus. The relief of my first steady job. The courage that surfaced when I faced setbacks and kept going anyway. Those glimmers were rarely dramatic, but they were enough. They reminded me that light often arrives in moments we easily overlook.

This chapter is about recognising those flickers and trusting that, even when the tunnel feels endless, you are not walking in vain. Resilience, faith and the willingness to notice what's working can transform the way forward. Sometimes, the very act of holding on becomes its own light.

We think of light as sudden and dazzling. More often, it's the steady courage of ordinary people who refuse to give up. Across history, countless people have walked long tunnels—through doubt, resistance and failure—before finding the light that changed their lives and those of others. Here are three such journeys.

One Cup of Vision, a Dash of Courage and a Generous Serving of Resilience

When we look closely at the stories of people who found their way through difficult seasons, three ingredients keep appearing: *vision*, *courage* and *resilience*.

Vision is the belief that change is possible, even when the world says otherwise.

Wangari Maathai saw this in action. Growing up in rural Kenya, she watched the forests that sustained her community disappear under deforestation. People told her one woman couldn't make a difference, but she held on to a bigger picture: a greener, stronger Kenya. She started planting trees, one by one, alongside other women who shared her dream. That small, consistent act became the Green Belt Movement, restoring millions of trees and empowering communities across the nation. Her story reminds us that vision begins quietly, with one person daring to see what could be.

Courage is taking the first small, brave step, even when fear whispers that you're not enough.

Rosa Parks embodied that spirit. She wasn't looking for fame or recognition; she was a Black woman and a seamstress who had spent years enduring the quiet, grinding weight of racial injustice. One ordinary evening in Montgomery, Alabama, she made an extraordinary choice: she refused to give up her seat to a white passenger. That single act of quiet defiance ignited the Montgomery Bus Boycott, uniting thousands in peaceful protest for over a year and becoming a turning point in the American civil rights movement. Courage doesn't always roar; it often speaks softly, in moments when we say, "No more."

Resilience is what keeps you walking when the path grows dark and uncertain.

Thomas Edison's persistence was legendary. He failed many times while trying to invent the light bulb, yet he refused to see those failures as proof of defeat. "I've not failed," he said, "I've just found 10,000 ways that won't work." With every attempt, he learnt, adjusted and tried again until light filled homes around the world. Resilience isn't about perfection—it's about choosing to keep going, no matter how long.

The beauty of these three ingredients is that they're not reserved for heroes in history books; they're available to all of us. You don't need permission, money or ideal conditions to use them. What you need is the willingness to believe that progress matters, even when it's invisible.

When your days feel heavy, resist the urge to add more

weight with negative stories or self-doubt. *Belief without action stays a dream, and action without belief collapses under pressure. It's the combination of both—holding a vision and moving towards it—that turns darkness into progress. Your belief whispers that light exists; your actions carve the path.*

Practical Recommendation: One Small, Consistent Action

When the tunnel feels endless, don't try to fix everything. Choose a simple action you can repeat daily:

- **At work:** Note one accomplishment at the end of each day. Patterns of progress emerge.

- **Wellbeing:** Take a ten-minute walk each morning. Let routine carry you when motivation won't.

- **Relationships:** Send one kind message each week. Connection lightens the load.

- **Big goals:** Like Edison, commit to one improvement a day. Even a miss is a step towards learning.

Stealing My Own Dream

Music has always held a special place in my life. It can flip my mood in seconds, spark creativity or calm my mind when I need to focus. Yet, despite loving it for years, I'd never learnt to play an instrument. Instead, I did what any clever parent might do—I tried to convince my son to learn classical guitar so one day he could serenade me with a beautiful song. Romantic idea, right? Well, he flat-out refused. Dream shattered. For a moment, I felt a little sad, as if that small fantasy had slipped through my fingers.

Then I thought, *Why should he have all the fun? What if I stole that dream and made it mine? I love music, I learn quickly, and honestly—why not?* So I enrolled at a nearby music academy, ordered a $60 guitar online and arrived ten minutes early for my first class. Bad timing: the teacher was still with an advanced student who sang and played piano like a pro. They were discussing notes as if they were speaking a secret language. I almost bolted, thinking, *What am I doing here?*

Finally, it was my turn. The teacher smiled and said, "I have two pieces of news—one good and one not so good. Which do you want first?" My nerves answered, "The bad one." He didn't sugarcoat it: "Your guitar is a toy. If you want to do this properly, you'll need a real instrument." Ouch. But then came the good news: "If you practise daily, you'll not only learn—you'll develop a deeper appreciation for music, because you'll understand what it takes to make it beautiful."

And so the adventure began: ten weeks of wrestling with strings, sore fingertips and calluses forming like tiny badges of honour. I ambitiously chose "Take On Me" by a-ha, thinking it looked simple. Big mistake. It demanded five lightning-fast chord changes—pure torture for hands more used to typing on a keyboard than playing solos. By the fourth class, I was ready to quit. "I need an easier song," I told my teacher. "I'll never get this in ten weeks." He shook his head. "No—you're further along than you think."

Then he proved it. He started playing alongside me, guiding me note by note, slowly at first, then faster. My fingers began to move almost on autopilot, and suddenly I realised: I was doing it. It was my *wax-on, wax-off* moment, straight out of *The Karate Kid*. Like Daniel polishing cars without knowing he was training, I'd been building muscle memory without realising it. The "impossible" song was beginning to live in my hands.

Learning guitar became a tunnel for me. At first, I held a vision—playing a song that once belonged to my son's dream—and that image kept me moving forward. Then came courage: showing up to class with a $60 guitar, pressing through sore fingers and self-doubt, daring to attempt something that felt impossible. Finally, I found resilience—pushing through frustration, trusting my teacher when I didn't trust myself, and realising that every callus and clumsy note was proof of progress.

Together, those three ingredients transformed what seemed like an endless struggle into a breakthrough. The exact recipe—vision, courage and resilience—applies to any challenging season we face in life.

What tunnel are you walking through right now, and how could you use vision, courage and resilience—one small step at a time—to find your own light at the end?

Sometimes, no matter how much vision, courage and resilience we muster, we still hit walls too heavy to move on our own. That's when we discover a strength that doesn't just come from within but beyond us: a quiet current running beneath our lives, ready to carry us forward when our own energy runs low.

Unlocking the Power Beyond Yourself

For some of us, the power that transcends our understanding looks like God or spiritual power. For others, it's the universe, the flow of life or simply the energy of people united by a shared purpose. Whatever name you give it, the idea is the same: there's something bigger than us to lean on when our own strength feels small. Think of it like Wi-Fi: you can't see it, you can't always explain how it works, but when you're connected, you suddenly have access to more than what's inside your own device.

And here's the thing: even those who proudly wear the "atheist" badge believe in something. Maybe not a God, but the power of human connection—their friends, their community, their champions who show up when life gets rough. Because no matter where we sit on the belief spectrum, we are wired to connect. We're social beings who draw courage, calm and clarity from others. Sometimes that connection feels divine; sometimes it feels purely human. But either way, it's proof that the beyond doesn't have to be mystical; it can be as simple as someone saying, "I'm here for you."

The real gift of tapping into this power, whether you call it God, the universe, community or compassion, is that it gives you space to breathe again. When you let go of your doubts, ask for help or simply speak your fears aloud, it's like cracking open a window in a stuffy room. Fresh air rushes in, and suddenly the tunnel doesn't feel so suffocating. That's how we unlock the power beyond ourselves: by daring to reach out, to trust and to believe that light doesn't live only inside us; it also shines through the connections, forces and mysteries that surround us.

Reflection: When was the last time you felt supported by something bigger than yourself, faith, nature, the universe or simply the kindness of people, and how could you lean on that source of strength again today?

A Moment of Connection

Imagine standing barefoot on the sand. The late-afternoon sun warms your skin, and a gentle breeze carries the salt of the sea and the scent of drying seaweed. Each breath feels like an invitation to let go and remember you're part of something vast and alive. As the waves roll in and retreat, your heartbeat falls into their rhythm, calm and confident. In that endless horizon, you sense a quiet presence, a reminder that life flows, renews and carries us forward even when we can't see the way. *That presence is the power beyond yourself—subtle but steady, reminding you that you're never walking alone.*

Sometimes that power doesn't arrive through sunsets or oceans; it shows up quietly, through people. Picture leaving the beach, still sandy-footed and lost in thought, when a stranger notices you juggling your things and smiles, holding the door open. Such a small act, almost ordinary, yet it softens the edges of your day. This is how the power beyond often moves—not in miracles but in *connection*.

The Power of Compassion

The most evident proof of the power beyond often comes not from grand miracles but from the raw, vulnerable moments of our own lives. I learnt this during one of my hardest chapters—when I had to reach out in a way that felt almost impossible for me.

My mother's insurance had almost run out after weeks of treatment to keep her breathing through COVID. I decided to create a GoFundMe campaign. I remember recording that first video, my voice trembling as I explained her situation. I pressed post, shared the link on my social media account and went to bed with a heavy heart—exhausted, hopeless and afraid that my prayer to see my mum strong again was slipping further away with each passing day.

The next day, I opened my inbox and froze. Messages from GoFundMe began flooding in: friends I hadn't spoken to in years, acquaintances I barely knew—even strangers had gathered around the campaign overnight with a generosity I had never expected. In that moment, the weight on my chest lifted, replaced by an almost electric warmth. It wasn't just the donations—it was the reminder that when life presses us down, others can and will lift us.

A few days later, my mother passed away. The funds helped with expenses, but the deeper gift was something I hadn't anticipated. For the first time, I truly felt the presence of a power beyond myself, alive in the kindness of others. It showed me how deeply we are connected, how compassion can turn strangers into a tribe and how, even in grief, we are never entirely alone.

Borrowing Courage: My Mother's Light

Yes, I've mentioned her many times throughout this book, but now I want you to truly meet her, not just as my mother but as the role model she was. She was the rock for my brothers and me. Sometimes she gave tough love, sometimes she was the patient teacher and sometimes she was the wise advisor whose words still echo in my heart. This is the story of my mother, **Ana Olivia**.

I still remember how she once got when I dedicated my high-achieving thesis to a university mentor instead of her. At the time, I didn't understand it, but now I do. This is my way of making amends for that moment—a small tribute, written entirely for her. My mum influenced our lives in more ways than I can count, guided always by her favourite saying: ***"Consistency and perseverance are the crowning glory of any achievement."*** And she proved it, not with speeches but with her life.

She was a single mother of three with no university education, yet she carried the fierce spirit of a South American woman who would never give up.

She began as a primary school teacher, one of the eldest of six children, working from a young age to help my grandmother keep the family afloat. When I look at photos of her youth, I see her playful smile, sparkling eyes and natural elegance. She once entered a beauty contest, and in the photo she kept in her bedroom, she looked radiant—jet-black hair, confident posture, a touch of Sophia Loren glamour straight out of the 60s.

But life demanded more than beauty. My father passed away young, at 49, after he and my mother had already divorced. Even then, she taught us to respect him. "He gave you life," she'd say, "and that alone deserves gratitude." Until midday, she taught at a local primary school, and after hours, she drove children home to earn extra money.

She was also a gifted artisan, creating delicate sculptures of saints and colourful Christmas ornaments. I sometimes wish I'd inherited her skill with her hands, but my craft turned out to be shaping ideas with words and numbers. She was always learning, always trying something new, always ensuring her children stayed on track. We didn't grow up with luxuries, but we had food in the fridge, bills paid and—most importantly—values that still guide my brothers and me today.

Of course, she had her moments of worry. Sometimes she

was angry when life pressed too hard. But what made her extraordinary was what came next; she always rose again. The next morning, she'd wake early, go to work and start all over. Again and again, until she reached her greatest triumph: standing proudly at the graduations of all three of her children, her sacrifices quietly stitched into every diploma.

As I began my own career, she and I often joined forces. Our relationship could be intense at times, but she always knew when I needed her wisdom. She didn't hold a bachelor's degree, but she had a doctorate in life, earned with honours. Her advice, her phrases, her example—they all live on in me, and now, through these words, I pass them on to you.

Because of her, I am here. Because of her, I can share this light with you. And who knows—perhaps through these pages, she's reaching you too, reminding you that every tunnel has a way out and that perseverance will carry you there.

Who in your life has been a model of perseverance and light—someone whose example reminds you that even in the darkest moments, it's possible to rise, keep going and reach the other side?

CARE: The Four Keys to Walking Any Tunnel

Looking back on the guitar lessons, the kindness of strangers and the painful courage of asking for help, I see the pieces of the CARE framework at work.

- **Comfort:** When we realise we're not alone—held by a smile, a community or something greater than ourselves—uncertainty feels a little safer to face.

- **Ambition:** Vision, courage and resilience live here. We stretch beyond fear and move towards purpose.

- **Renewal:** We recharge through music, nature and connection, giving us the energy to continue.

- **Equilibrium:** Life keeps moving. Balance isn't perfection; it's weaving comfort, ambition and renewal into a workable rhythm.

The tunnel may not change its length, but with CARE, you become the source of light that guides you through.

Practical CARE in Everyday Life

Turn the framework into weekly muscle memory.

- **Comfort (Mon/Tue):** Schedule time with a person or space that feels safe. If that's not possible, create micro-comfort: five deep breaths, a favourite tea, a no-phones walk.

- **Ambition (Wed/Thu):** Choose one stretch for the week and break it into two tiny steps. Celebrate completion, not size.

- **Renewal (Fri/Sat):** Plan one reliable refill—music, ocean air, a book in the sun. Treat it as a non-negotiable.

- **Equilibrium (Sun):** Review your week. *What needs softening? What needs structure?* Remove one unnecessary obligation. Add one small support.

Over time, rhythm becomes instinct. Instinct carries you through hard seasons.

Bringing It All Together: Key Takeaways

When the tunnel feels endless, it's easy to believe the light has disappeared. But as we've seen, light rarely bursts in all at once; it arrives in fragments. A kind gesture, a small success or a spark of courage to keep going can shift everything. Whether through the resilience of Wangari Maathai, the quiet defiance of Rosa Parks or Edison's relentless experimentation, we're reminded that change begins with small, consistent acts of vision, courage and persistence.

I've learnt that same lesson in my own tunnels—through learning guitar when it felt impossible, through the humbling experience of asking for help during my mother's illness and through the countless ways others have held me when I couldn't hold myself together. Each experience showed me that light is not only found at the end of the tunnel; it grows within us as we walk, and it's magnified by the people and forces that walk beside us.

Every small act of belief, courage or kindness brightens the way, proving that no tunnel lasts forever, and the journey itself can become the source of light we've been searching for.

"CONSISTENCY AND PERSEVERANCE ARE THE CROWNING GLORY OF ANY ACHIEVEMENT."

Ana Oliva Arellano Contreras

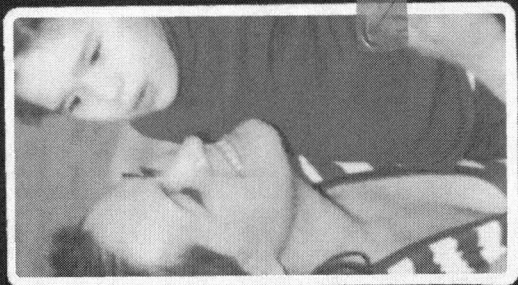

STEALING MY OWN DREAM

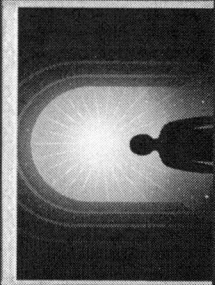

MY MOTHER'S LIGHT

ETERNAL LOVE

Chapter Eight

Unbreakable Bond—The Relationship with Yourself

There's one person you'll spend every moment of your life with—and it's not your partner, your kids or your boss. It's you. From the moment you take your first breath until your very last, there is one constant presence in your life: *you*. The bond you hold with yourself is the foundation on which everything else is built. It's the lens through which you interpret the world, the voice that whispers in your quiet moments and the anchor that steadies you when life feels uncertain.

Neglecting this relationship means drifting through life disconnected from your most trustworthy source of strength. Self-awareness unlocks your potential and helps you live with purpose. Yet, few of us are ever taught how to nurture that bond. We learn how to love others, succeed and fit in, but rarely are we encouraged to explore what it truly means to know, accept and stand by ourselves.

Building an unbreakable bond with yourself isn't about perfection or relentless positivity—it's about cultivating honesty, compassion and resilience in the relationship that will outlast every other. *When you begin to see yourself as both your own companion and guide, life opens up with greater clarity and meaning.* The journey of self-discovery isn't always easy, but it's always worth it.

The Questions We Avoid

We all have those questions we quietly tiptoe around, that sit in the back of our minds like uninvited guests at a barbecue. You know the ones—*Am I really happy?* and *Is this what I actually want to be doing with my life?*

Instead of facing them, we distract ourselves with busyness, food or shopping. *Why?* Because deep down, we suspect the answers might nudge us out of our comfort zone, and let's be honest, that zone has really comfy cushions.

But here's the secret: the very questions you avoid are the ones holding the keys to your next breakthrough. Try asking, "Am I being true to my values?" or "Am I living a life that aligns with what I care about most?"

Reflection: Write down one question you've been avoiding. What makes it uncomfortable? What might change if you answered it?

The Truth You'd Rather Not Ask Yourself

It's far easier to scroll, snack or binge-watch something than to sit quietly and wonder, *Am I actually happy with where I'm going?* Why poke around in a cupboard you suspect is full of spiders, right?

But here's the twist: when you finally look, you often find it's not a spider at all—just an old sock you forgot about. The longer you avoid those moments of reflection, the bigger and scarier they seem.

We also dodge situations that make us feel insecure, as if insecurity were contagious. Instead of leaning in, we run from them, whispering, "Better safe than sorry." But safety, while cosy, can become a trap. Growth doesn't happen in the comfort zone—it occurs in those awkward, slightly sweaty-palmed moments when you risk failing, stumbling or discovering that you don't have it all figured out. Spoiler: nobody does.

And then there's the big one: what you really want in life. It's the kind of question that makes most of us quietly back away. Why? Because admitting what you want means facing the possibility that you're not living it yet. And that takes courage.

But exploring your true ambition doesn't mean overhauling your life overnight. It starts small—admitting, "I've always dreamed of doing this thing ..." The more you honour that voice, the lighter it feels.

I know what it feels like to avoid those questions. For years, I did precisely that.

The Wake-Up Call I Couldn't Ignore

I know that feeling well. On paper, my career looked seamless: local roles, then regional responsibilities and eventually a global function. It all looked impressive. But underneath the surface? There were plenty of days when I'd catch myself daydreaming about something completely different—writing, sharing my thoughts, connecting with people beyond job titles—a bit like craving chocolates while you're still halfway through your fish and three veggies.

I recall sitting in a meeting, pretending to focus, when my mind was preoccupied with the book I wanted to write. That moment was a wake-up call. Over time, I realised what I enjoyed most about my work wasn't the strategies or spreadsheets—it was the people: helping my team recognise their strengths, encouraging them to find solutions and sparking new ideas with peers.

That's when it dawned on me: this was a gift. I just hadn't seen it as one at the time.

Then, as life does, it threw a few curveballs my way, forcing me to offer myself the same encouragement I'd always given others. Some days I couldn't see my own strengths clearly (funny how easy it is to cheer everyone else on but forget to back yourself). Slowly, I began tuning my inner compass—what I now call my CARE puzzle—into my own little experiment in balance.

That framework helped me recover faster from challenges and eventually inspired this book.

Reflection: What parts of your day make you lose track of time or feel most alive? Those moments might be whispering clues about your deeper purpose.

Conversations in the Mirror

Most of us have a running commentary in our heads that could win awards for drama, sarcasm or creative insults. You know that moment when you catch your reflection and think, *Wow, I really need more sleep ... and maybe a personal stylist*? Yep, we all do it.

The trouble is, this internal banter isn't just background noise; it shapes how we see ourselves and how we show up in the world. Imagine if you spoke to your friends the way you some-times talk to yourself. You'd probably lose a few friends fast.

The good news? You can change the script. Start by notic-ing the "soundtrack" running in your head and flipping it to something kinder.

That little voice in your head isn't the enemy—it's just loud. Sometimes it cheers you on, but often it's a harsh com-mentator: "Nice try, but you'll probably stuff it up again!"

You can't silence it entirely, but you can change your relation-ship with it. Think of it like turning down a cranky neighbour while turning up the playlist you actually enjoy. By learning a few simple techniques, you can catch that negative chatter before it takes over—and replace it with something far more helpful.

Everyday Techniques That Work

Catch It, Name It, Flip It

I once muttered, "You're hopeless at this," while knitting a sweater. To be fair, the instructions didn't make much sense. Instead of spiralling, I stopped and said, "Ah, there's my critic again." Then I flipped it to, "Okay, this is fiddly, but you've handled tougher puzzles." Suddenly, it felt like a challenge, not a failure.

The Mate Test

Imagine saying to your best mate, "You'll never pull this off—you're just not good enough." You wouldn't, right? Next time your inner critic speaks up, run it through the Mate Test: *Would I say this to a friend?* If not, reframe it with kindness.

Sticky-Note Nudges

A friend of mine has sticky notes everywhere: on her mirror, kettle and even her laptop. At first, I thought she'd gone overboard. Then I read them: *Talk to yourself like someone you love. Progress, not perfection.* Tiny reminders like these act as circuit breakers for negative self-talk.

The "Done" List

Instead of listing what you didn't finish, write down what you did—sent that tough email. Cooked dinner. Went for a walk. It shifts your focus from lack to progress, rewiring your brain to celebrate effort over perfection.

Two-Minute Pause

During a stressful meeting, I once felt the spiral coming on— *You're not making sense. Everyone's judging you.* I took a two-minute break, splashed water on my face and breathed deeply. I came back calmer, clearer and more grounded. Negative self-talk thrives on speed—a pause slows it down.

Gratitude with a Twist

We all know about gratitude lists. Why not add *yourself* to the list? *I'm grateful I showed up even though I was tired. I'm grateful I called a friend.* It feels awkward at first, but it teaches you to notice your own effort.

Reflection: Choose one of these techniques and practise it today. Notice how your inner voice shifts—even a minor tweak counts as progress.

At the End of the Day

The longest relationship you'll ever have is the one you have with yourself. You can change jobs, countries or even the people around you, but you can't swap the person looking back in the mirror.

That's why this bond matters so much. It's not about silencing every doubt. It's about learning to listen, question, be honest and—most importantly—be kind.

When you face uncomfortable truths, you open the door to growth. When you change the conversation in your head, you reshape how you experience life. And *when you treat yourself with the same compassion you give others, you stop being your own obstacle and start becoming your greatest ally.*

So, here's your invitation: start small. Ask one brave question. Catch one harsh thought and flip it to something kinder. Celebrate one small win before the day ends. These aren't just habits; they're stepping stones towards a deeper connection with yourself.

Because once you strengthen that bond, everything else—your relationships, your work, your dreams—begins to align more naturally.

The relationship you have with yourself sets the tone for your whole life.

Imagine the ripple effect if you became your own greatest ally. What doors would open? What dreams might finally feel possible?

Bringing It All Together: Key Takeaways

The most enduring relationship you'll ever have is the one you share with yourself. This chapter reminds us that self-connection isn't a luxury; it's the foundation of everything else. When you learn to know yourself, listen to your needs and treat yourself with the same compassion you offer others, life begins to feel steadier, more genuine and more fulfilling.

Facing the hard questions—*Am I happy? Am I living in line with my values? What do I truly want?*—is not easy, but it's where growth begins. Those uncomfortable reflections are less about judgement and more about curiosity; they help uncover what lights you up and what's quietly asking for change. The stories of patiently knitting a sweater or craving something "more" show how listening to your inner voice can quietly guide you back to what feels meaningful.

This chapter reminds us that our relationship with ourselves shapes everything else—our choices, our confidence, our joy. When we start treating ourselves with curiosity and kindness, we make space for growth, courage and meaning. Through simple daily techniques like *Catch it, Name it, Flip it* and the *Mate Test*, you can learn to shift your self-talk, slow down negative spirals and build a more grounded sense of confidence. Strengthening that unbreakable bond with yourself doesn't happen overnight; it occurs in small, consistent acts of kindness and awareness that add up over time.

EXPLORING NEW PATHS

CURIOUS

LISTENING TO MY VOICE

STRONGER

WHEN YOU TREAT YOURSELF WITH THE SAME COMPASSION YOU GIVE OTHERS, YOU STOP BEING YOUR OWN OBSTACLE AND START BECOMING YOUR GREATEST ALLY.

Fatima

Part Three

Breaking Free, Never Looking Back

Part Three

Breaking Free, Never Looking Back

In Part One, we unpacked the early noise—the voices of doubt, old labels and stories that once shaped how you saw yourself. Part Two helped you reconnect with your values, clear out emotional clutter and tune back into what truly matters. Now, in Part Three, it's time to bring that inner work to life. This is where change becomes visible—where your growth starts to ripple through your everyday choices and moments.

We begin by learning to hold your ground with *Sorry, Not Sorry: Boundaries with Grace*. Here, you'll discover how to say no—without guilt, without tension—and protect your time and energy. You'll find your voice: steady, calm and kind, yet firm enough to protect your peace. Boundaries aren't barriers; they're invitations for healthier connections and more authentic living.

From there, we move into *Renewal & Self-Care: A Journey to Your True Voice*. Once you've created space by saying no to what drains you, this chapter will help you say yes to what restores you. It's not about indulgence—it's about intention. Through simple, meaningful habits, you'll nurture stillness, ease and strength. You'll feel steady in your body, anchored in your mind and reconnected with your sense of self.

With that grounding, we'll explore *Redefining Your Relationship with Money*—an area that quietly influences so much of how we live and feel. Together, we'll let go of the guilt, pressure and old stories that shape your money mindset. You'll look at your patterns and beliefs with curiosity, not criticism, and begin rewriting the story so that money becomes a tool for freedom, rather than a source of stress.

Finally, *Next-Level You: Rise, Reset, Reinvent* is about embracing reinvention—not because life forces your hand but because you choose it. You'll walk through a ten-step process designed to help you shift with clarity, courage and intention—on your own terms. This isn't about becoming someone new; it's about stepping fully into who you already are.

Together, these chapters form your practical toolkit for living lighter, leading with intention and backing yourself completely. Whether you're learning to say "no" with grace, carving out moments to recharge, reshaping your money story or redefining what's next, this is where your inner clarity begins to shape your outer world.

You don't have to change everything overnight. Each slight shift builds momentum—each decision, each boundary, each moment of honesty adds up. Before you know it, you'll feel more grounded, more aligned and more in charge of the life you're creating.

Let's keep going—you're closer than you think. Every bit of courage you've built so far is lighting the way for what's next.

Chapter Nine

Sorry, Not Sorry— Boundaries With Grace

Have you felt the relief of setting a boundary? It's like being the security guard of your own life—velvet rope up, guest list in hand—deciding who gets in, who waits and who's not on the list.

The trouble is, most of us hand that list to anyone with a friendly smile. Suddenly, your cruisy Saturday becomes moving a mate's couch, minding your cousin's kelpie and answering work emails while your flat white turns stone-cold.

Here's the truth: boundaries aren't rude or selfish; they protect you from becoming an all-you-can-eat buffet of time, energy and emotional labour. Think fences—not spiky "keep out" barriers but a white-picket fence with a friendly gate.

A reasonable boundary is like a sign on your door: *I like you—please knock*. Without it, life turns into a backyard barbie where everyone rocks up, brings their drama and forgets the potato salad.

Done well, boundaries aren't harsh—they're easy-going, even elegant. It's not slamming doors; it's a calm "nah, I'm good" delivered as casually as "pass the salt". Think of them as lending someone your favourite bracelet: not everyone gets to borrow it, and when they do, you trust they'll take care of it and return it in good shape. The goal isn't to keep people out; it's to make sure that what you share—your time, energy and warmth—goes where it's valued and respected.

Saying "no" can feel awkward, like turning down a neighbour's invite when you'd rather stay in your pyjamas. But it doesn't need a grand speech. It can be as simple as stirring milk into your tea—steady, kind, no fuss. In a world of constant demands, no is fresh air: a moment of freedom, a step towards self-respect and a quiet reminder that your needs matter too. Boundaries aren't about picking fights—they're about choosing where to invest your care.

Sometimes the most powerful thing you can serve is a polite no. It's not weakness; it's strength and self-respect. *Your limits deserve as much respect as your generosity—and honouring them is what keeps both intact.*

The Power of "No"

People often confuse assertiveness with confrontation, but real assertiveness is simply being honest in a respectful way. It's about speaking up without putting anyone down. When you bring that mindset into boundary-setting, "no" stops feeling harsh and becomes a calm statement of your limits.

You're not being difficult—you're being clear. And that clarity is kindness—to you and to them.

The constant "yes" habit is exhausting. It feeds stress, burnout and quiet resentment towards the people you're trying to please. Boundaries are your guardrails: they keep you steady, protect your energy and give you room to breathe. Every time you say "no" to something that drains you, you're saying "yes" to peace of mind and balance.

Of course, not everyone will welcome your boundaries. Some will push back or play the guilt card. The trick is to stay calm and consistent. Picture yourself as a lighthouse in a storm—steady and visible, no matter how rough the waves get.

A few simple strategies can help.

- **Broken record:** Repeat your "no" calmly and consistently—"That doesn't work for me." or "I won't be able to take that on right now." No excuses needed.

- **Acknowledge and redirect:** Show empathy, then hold your ground—"I know this matters to you, but I need to stick to my limits. Let's explore another option."

- **Buy time:** "Let me think about that and get back to you." This gives you space to decide without pressure or guilt.

Remember, your first responsibility is to yourself, not to managing someone else's reaction. Over time, people learn that your boundaries are real and adjust accordingly. Those who don't? That says more about them than about you.

And let's be honest—sometimes we're the ones crossing lines. Coaxing a tired mate for "just one drink" or asking a colleague to take on "a quick task" might seem harmless, but it chips away at trust. Respect is like Vegemite—spread too thin and it loses its punch. *Respecting boundaries, both ours and others', is what keeps relationships balanced and genuine.*

Being on the receiving end of a bulldozed boundary stings. It's not just about the extra task—it's the unspoken message: *your no doesn't matter.* When that happens repeatedly, it erodes confidence and fosters resentment.

So here's the choice: value self-respect or cave to convenience. A boundary isn't a wall; it's a fair line. When we honour it, we build trust, clarity and peace. Next time you're tempted to push past someone's "no", picture yourself gate-crashing their backyard barbie—piling your plate high and asking where dessert is. Funny in theory, but exhausting in practice. *Respect, when shared, is always the better dish to serve.*

Corporate Boundaries, Personal Balance

Balancing boundaries in the corporate world can feel like juggling hot chips while holding a flat white—one wrong move and you're burned, stressed or cleaning up a mess. We've all been there: endless meetings, "urgent" requests landing at 5:59 pm and polite nodding when you'd rather be saying "not possible".

Workplace boundaries aren't about being difficult; they're about staying sane and helping projects run smoothly without everyone running on fumes. When done well, they turn chaos into collaboration—and make Monday mornings a little less daunting.

Anyone who's worked in a busy team knows that setting boundaries can feel risky, like playing with fire. I've been there too. Saying "no" or holding your ground can seem like you're stepping out of line, but the truth is, boundaries at work don't need to be dramatic. When projects have realistic timelines and open communication, boundaries almost take care of themselves. Everyone knows what to expect, and no one feels blindsided.

The trouble is that ideals rarely last. Projects shift, timelines shrink and last-minute requests pile up like unread emails when returning from holidays. I once worked with a team that said "yes" to every demand. Deadlines became impossible, people worked late nights, and in the end, the project still launched late—and poorly. No one dared to set limits, and the outcome showed it. ***Ignoring boundaries didn't just harm wellbeing—it hurt the business.***

A healthy workplace starts with respect for limits. Leaders need to value realistic timelines, colleagues need to recognise each other's workloads and everyone needs the courage to be upfront about capacity—without guilt. When boundaries are handled well, they create space for honesty, smoother collaboration and a shift from competition to genuine teamwork. Boundaries protect individuals—but they also strengthen the whole group.

One smart way to do this is to align roles with people's strengths and time zones. Imagine a global team where an early riser in Sydney handles the first wave of updates, while a night owl in Europe picks it up in a smooth handover. Suddenly, projects move seamlessly around the clock without burning anyone out. Likewise, letting detail-orientated people own the planning while big-picture thinkers lead strategy means everyone plays to their strengths.

After years of working across global teams, I've seen both the challenges and the incredible potential of cross-border collaboration. When done with clarity and purpose, this approach makes boundaries almost effortless. People feel less stretched because the work fits their natural rhythm. Time zones shift from headache to advantage, and handovers run smoothly. Most importantly, people feel heard and valued—their strengths aren't being overlooked; they're being well used. The result? Sustainable, energising project cultures with fewer late-night emails/meetings and far more momentum.

How to Align Roles with Strengths and Time Zones

- **Map the team early:** Kick off projects by learning each stakeholder's preferred working style, strengths and time zone. A quick survey or workshop can reveal patterns that prevent clashes later.

- **Match roles to strengths:** Planners should track schedules, visionaries should guide strategy and relationship-builders should manage engagement. Matching people to the work that suits them not only reduces friction and helps boundaries stick—it also brings a sense of professional fulfilment and flow. When people play to their strengths, work feels lighter, more meaningful and naturally more effective.

- **Use time zones as a relay:** Treat the workflow like a way to share the load from one person to the next. Clear handovers and status updates ensure the project keeps moving, even when no one logs in at midnight.

- **Review and adjust:** Boundaries aren't static. Check in at milestones to tweak workloads and handovers. Flexibility shows respect for changing circumstances and helps maintain momentum.

Boundaries don't just live in boardrooms and project plans—they show up in our personal lives too, often in the most unexpected ways. Just as deadlines, workloads and stakeholder expectations in the corporate world test how well we draw the line, so do the people closest to us. Sometimes the clearest lessons about balance and respect don't come from workplace manuals or leadership books but from the everyday moments of family life. In fact, one of my most powerful lessons about boundaries didn't come from a manager or mentor—it came from my niece.

What My Niece Taught Me About Boundaries

When she first arrived in Australia for uni, everything felt foreign to her—new language, systems, even the city feeling. I became her shortcut to settling in: taking her shopping, showing her around, laughing through cultural hiccups. Somewhere along the way, she stopped being just my niece and became my companion, my best mate and, in some ways, my daughter.

Those first two years were rough on her, just like they'd been on me when I arrived. I knew the script: the confusion over slang (try explaining *arvo*), the homesickness and that awkward feeling of being a guest in your own new life. So I told her straight: "Give it two years—you'll find your rhythm."

Then it happened. Out of the blue, she slipped into her own skin as if it had been waiting for her all along. She graduated, built her circle of friends and landed her first job. The girl who had once clung to me at the shops was now heading to after-work drinks without needing me to translate

Aussie banter. I was thrilled—though a bit wistful, because I'd grown very comfortable in my role as the all-knowing aunt-slash-mother figure.

But life had other plans. She found her voice, packed her bags and moved out. In that moment, she drew her first real boundary—not with rebellion but with quiet confidence, saying, "I'm not a girl anymore." I'd be lying if I said it didn't sting. Part of me wanted to tuck her back under my wing. But then it clicked: I'd done my job. I'd given her everything she needed to fly. *The real win wasn't keeping her close—it was watching her soar, capable, confident and completely herself.*

That's when I realised boundaries aren't walls—they're proof that lessons stuck. And I just hope she still remembers who showed her where to find the best pies in Sydney (no doubt, Pittwater Rd in Collaroy).

Watching her step into her own life taught me something I didn't expect: **boundaries create space for growth.** Her decision to move out and stand tall wasn't rejection—it was the clearest sign she was living what I'd shared. Boundaries gave her wings, and they gave me the grace to let go. In the end, the power of boundaries isn't about holding on—it's about stepping back, so love can evolve into respect and independence.

Energy Saved Is Energy Earned

We like to pretend we can do it all. Spoiler: we can't. Running on empty isn't a badge of honour—it's a fast track to grumpiness, wobbly decisions and that special kind of fatigue where even choosing a Netflix show feels like hard labour. Protecting your energy isn't about doing more; it's about doing less, better.

If you're flat out all morning without a pause, you'll be running on fumes by lunch.

One of the simplest ways to recharge is to delegate. *Yes, that word.* Delegation isn't shirking—it's sharing. Every time you hand over a task—at work, at home or in your community—you're not being lazy; you're being strategic. Save your energy for the things only you can do. Imagine conducting an orchestra: if you tried to play every instrument yourself, the music would fall apart and you'd pass out before the first chorus. Delegation lets the music flow—while you still have enough breath to enjoy it.

Energy-saving doesn't just live in the office. It shows up everywhere—especially in everyday life. Maybe it's leaving the party after two hours instead of soldiering on till midnight. Perhaps it's choosing a walk-and-talk with a friend over a three-hour dinner, or giving yourself permission to mute the group chat and enjoy the silence. At work, it might mean blocking focus time so back-to-back meetings don't swallow your day. It might mean choosing three priorities instead of twelve, or actually taking your lunch away from the desk so your brain remembers what oxygen feels like. These choices look ordinary, but they're powerful energy savers—and energy saved is energy earned.

Delegation belongs at home, too. Teach the kids to fold laundry (it won't be perfect, but neither is burnout). You don't always have to be the one who organises the group hangout. Sharing the load provides others a chance to step up—and gives you room to breathe.

Of course, delegation sounds excellent in theory and tricky in practice. Handing something over can feel risky. *What if they don't do it right? What if it comes back worse?*

Or—*What if they do it better?* Cue that inner whisper: *It's quicker if I do it. At least it'll be done properly. People rely on me to consistently deliver.* Familiar?

Here's the catch: that inner dialogue isn't really about the task—it's about trust and control. When we refuse to delegate, we're telling ourselves our worth is tied to doing everything personally. Secret belief: *If I don't hold it all together, everything will fall apart.* But you and I both know that's not true. Clutching every responsibility doesn't make you more capable—it just makes you more exhausted. And exhaustion isn't a medal; it's a warning light.

So ask yourself: *What story do I tell when I won't delegate? No one else can handle it? I don't want to burden anyone. I'll become irrelevant if I'm not the do-it-all person?* Be honest—it's probably a mix. The good news is that spotting the script is the first step to rewriting it. **Delegation doesn't mean "I can't". It means "I don't have to do it alone". That shift—from control to collaboration—is where the real energy savings begin.**

Practical: Your Personal Energy Audit

Sometimes the fastest way to protect your energy is simply noticing what (or who) is draining it. Think of this as an audit for your life—not your tax return (blissfully, it involves less paperwork).

Audit your relationships

- List the people you spend the most time with.
- Next to each name, ask: *Do I feel lighter or heavier after seeing them, energised or drained?* You don't have to cut people off.

- You do get to set better boundaries—or invest more in the ones who genuinely lift you.

News & social media fasts

- Try a 24-hour break (your phone will survive).
- Notice the shift: more calm, less comparison, more time?
- Decide your rhythm—weekly, monthly or whenever your brain feels stuck on doomscroll.

Choose uplifting inputs

- Fill the gaps with something nourishing: a podcast that inspires, music that lifts your mood or a book that stretches your thinking.
- Your mind's a garden—if you don't plant flowers, the weeds move in.

Set an "energy budget"

- Like money, decide where your daily energy goes: work, family, creativity, health.
- If it doesn't fit the budget, it's probably time to say "no" or delegate.

Now, before you think all this talk about saving energy and delegation is just theory, let me share a story. It doesn't involve boardrooms or corporate deadlines—it involves my son, a school project and one of the strangest shapes you'll ever meet: the dodecahedron. Yes, even a twelve-sided polygon can teach us a thing or two about energy and delegation.

The Dodecahedron

Pop quiz: Do you remember what a dodecahedron is? I didn't—until my son stormed in looking like the world had ended because he had to build a project around one. He wasn't the only frustrated party. Cue family delegation: this homework just became a team sport.

Our first move? A stealth investigation. *Wikipedia. Google.* A deep dive into platonic solids. After overdosing on "12-sided shape" jargon, I presented my grand discovery. My son blinked. Yawned. The dodecahedron landed with all the excitement of a wet sock. That's when it clicked—it wasn't about the maths; it was about energy. How could we make this thing enjoyable?

So we turned to the oracle: *YouTube.* There we found a cracker of a tutorial on turning dodecahedra into geometric art. Suddenly, the project shifted from a tedious slog to a creative challenge. His frustration turned into curiosity. *The lesson? When life hands you a dull dodecahedron, add curiosity, a dash of creativity and some fun.* Tedious tasks don't have to stay tedious—connect them to what sparks energy for you.

Looking back, the dodecahedron wasn't really about geometry—it was about energy and collaboration. I could've muscled through solo, but instead we shared the load, laughed through the confusion and found a way to make it fun. **That's the magic of delegation: it doesn't just save energy—it multiplies it.** When you bring others in, especially in ways that connect to what excites them, the "ugh" jobs get lighter and far more memorable.

So next time you're staring at your own version of a dodecahedron—a dull report, a never-ending to-do list or a tricky project—ask yourself: *Who can I bring in, and how can we make this more energising?* Sometimes the most brilliant move isn't to do more—it's to share more. And if all else fails, there's always *YouTube*.

Pause, Filter, Freedom

Real freedom is choosing what gets in. Before you say yes, pause. Ask: *Do I want this? Does it fit my priorities?* That minor breach between motivation and action is your power.

Treat it like a spam filter: not every request deserves access to the inbox.

Practical Ways to Practise It

- 24-hour (or 24-minute) rule: Buy time before committing.

- Check your energy bank: If this "yes" steals sleep or sanity, it's a "no".

- Use tech as an ally: Batch emails, silence notifications, put your phone away while you recharge.

- Go-to pause phrases:
    - "Let me check my schedule and get back to you."
    - "I'll need some time to think that over."
    - "I'm not sure right now, but I'll let you know."

- Curate your circle: More of who lifts you, less of who drains you.

- Micro-pauses: Taking a five-second pause before replying can reset an entire day.

Bringing It All Together: Key Takeaways

Boundaries don't shut people out—they make space for what matters. From the quiet power of a graceful "no" to protecting your mental health and energy, balance comes when you stop trying to do it all. At work and at home, boundaries are anchors when expectations start to pull.

Delegation, pausing and filtering remind us that freedom isn't about more—it's about *better*. Even a school project on a dodecahedron proves it: share the load, inject curiosity, and the dull becomes memorable. Boundaries aren't just fences; they're doorways to respect, collaboration and a lighter way of living.

THE DODECAHEDRON

MY NIECE TAUGHT ME ABOUT BOUNDARIES

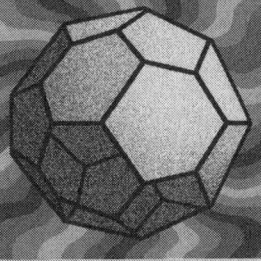

YOUR LIMITS DESERVE AS MUCH RESPECT AS YOUR GENEROSITY—AND HONOURING THEM IS WHAT KEEPS BOTH INTACT.

Fatima

Chapter Ten

Renewal & Self-Care—A Journey to Your True Voice

Sometimes the only "me time" you get in a day is brushing your teeth while checking emails or eating lunch at your desk, pretending reheated leftovers are a five-star experience. If that sounds familiar, it's time to recognise you are due for a daily dose of *you*. Self-care is a necessity, and it's not selfish to prioritise yourself. Your wellbeing isn't just important; it's vital to affirm your worth, and that makes you feel more significant in your own life.

Life has a sneaky way of filling up—like that one kitchen drawer we all have where batteries, rubber bands and mystery keys retire. Our minds are no different. We store worries, replay old conversations and pile up "shoulds" as if we're auditioning for an episode of Mental Hoarders. The result? A cluttered mind with no room for clarity, creativity or joy.

But imagine if you gave yourself permission—just a few

minutes a day—to pause, breathe and actually check in with yourself. To listen not to the endless to-do list but to how you feel, what you need and what might make you laugh. This is the part of you that often gets neglected, the part quietly asking for care and attention.

Think of it as spring cleaning for the mind: clearing out the dusty doubts, the stale guilt and that nagging voice that whispers, "you're not doing enough", and letting in lightness, calm and clarity. You can start small: take a morning walk, write a few lines in a journal or simply sit still for five minutes. These little acts clear mental clutter and create space for focus, energy and freedom.

Take this as your invitation to declutter not just your physical space but your headspace. To take your daily dose of you without guilt—if you can find time to charge your phone, you can find time to recharge yourself.

A busy mind feels like a noisy intersection at peak hour—horns blaring, lights flashing, people rushing and you stuck in the middle, unsure where to go. A still mind, on the other hand, is like sitting beside a quiet lake at dawn: calm, expansive, full of possibility.

That's not just poetic—it's science. Mindfulness and meditation have been shown to reduce blood pressure and stress hormones while sharpening memory and focus. Something as simple as slow breathing or a five-minute meditation can make a big difference. A still mind isn't just pleasant—it's medicine.

When clarity leads, the world doesn't just get quieter—it gets kinder. Clarity strengthens decision-making, deepens relationships and creates ease in everyday life. When your mind is clear, your words land, your choices align and you feel in control. This calm confidence helps you navigate life's challenges with a steady hand.

Clarity is the windscreen wiper; your voice is the driver. Without wiping away the fog, you can't see where you're heading. But clear the screen, and suddenly the road opens up—direction becomes obvious, confidence builds and your voice leads the way. Finding your voice isn't about volume—it's about removing the static so that when you speak, it carries warmth, weight and authenticity.

And here's the truth: *when your voice becomes clearer through mental clarity, it's not just about sharper choices or better chats—it's about protecting the core of who you are.* Because at the end of the day, your mental health underpins everything. Without it, even the best plans can wobble. With it, everything else—relationships, work, creativity—has the solid ground it needs to thrive.

Mind, Mental Health and Physical Health: Distinct but Connected

Imagine your mind as a busy café on the corner of town. Inside, conversations never stop—some cheerful, some anxious, some just noisy. At one table sit your memories, at another your worries, ordering round after round, and in a quiet corner your dreams whisper. That café is your mind—lively, crowded, always buzzing.

Mental health is the atmosphere of the café. On a good day, the lighting is warm, the air is fresh and the chatter feels light. On a tough day, the music is too loud, the air is heavy and you just want to leave. The conversations haven't changed, but how you experience them has—and that's the way mental health shows up in action.

When your mental health is cared for—like cleaning the café, opening the windows and keeping the noise in check—you create a space where your mind can function without chaos. Thoughts flow, emotions settle and your inner voice can be heard. Neglect it, and the café becomes cluttered and overwhelming, obscuring your clarity.

Your mind, mental health and physical health (body) are like three musicians in the same band—when one's off-key, the whole song stumbles. *The mind directs, mental health balances and physical health gives rhythm.* Stress can tighten your shoulders, but strong mental health can calm a racing heart and physical vitality can lift your mood. They're not separate players but an ensemble—nurture one, and the others find their harmony.

When physical health falters, it's like losing the drummer—the beat collapses, everything feels heavier and even small tasks become mountainous. Research shows that lack of sleep or chronic illness heighten stress, blur thinking and increase anxiety or depression. The body isn't a shell—it's your partner in balance. When it struggles, the echo is felt everywhere.

When Mind and Body Collide

I know this firsthand. Weeks before my wedding, my boyfriend—now husband—became suddenly ill. What doctors first thought was appendicitis turned out to be Crohn's disease, a chronic inflammatory condition of the digestive tract. The diagnosis shook our world. Overnight, he faced not just physical pain but the emotional toll Crohn's brings—anxiety, depression, isolation.

Those early days were brutal. Marriage, migration and managing his illness all collided. His mood was tested daily, and there were countless emergency visits. I watched him take morphine for pain so intense that even that wasn't enough. Then came a turning point. One night, a doctor explained that Crohn's wasn't just a physical fight—it was a mental one as well. To make it clear, he compared life with Crohn's to *Mortal Kombat*. Each choice either weakened him, giving the opponent power, or strengthened him, keeping him in the game. My husband realised he held the controller.

From then on, he made different choices: he improved his nutrition, ran to release anger, chose less stressful work, slowed his pace and found joy in small things. Gradually, his health transformed. The pain eased, his symptoms faded and the emergency visits stopped. It's been seventeen years since his last admission.

The lesson? ***Healing isn't only about treating the body—it's about nurturing the mind. Recovery begins with the desire for a better outcome and the daily choices that support it.***

7 Quick Actions You Can Take Today

You don't need a grand plan or a week off overseas to reset your energy. Real renewal starts with small, intentional actions—the kind that take minutes, not hours. Try these today.

For Your Mind & Space

1. Start a mini ritual: Light a candle, brew a cuppa or set a straightforward intention.

2. Protect your rest: Go to bed 30 minutes earlier or take lunch outside, phone-free.

3. Clear one spot: Tidy your desk, bedside table or kitchen bench.

For Your Body

1. Move: Walk briskly, dance or stretch while the kettle boils.

2. Hydrate: Swap coffee or a soft drink for water.

3. Fuel simply: Add one extra serve of fruit or veg to your meals.

4. Book a health check: Prevention is always easier than repair.

Your future self will thank you for every small step you take today.

Joy, Play and Gratitude: Your Daily Compass

There comes a point when success, checklists and obligations no longer satisfy, and you start asking: *What truly lights me up?* That's where joy steps in—not as a fleeting thrill but as a compass. When you let joy guide you, it points you towards choices, people and paths that feel true. It's less about chasing the "right" direction and more about following what feels alive.

Joy doesn't need to be grand. It's not winning the lottery or buying a car—it's the little sparks: laughing at a silly joke, savouring a coffee or dancing in the kitchen while dinner cooks. Choosing joy means noticing those sparks and leaning into them instead of rushing past. They're breadcrumbs leading you home.

Play is joy's cheeky sidekick, and somewhere between paying bills and answering emails, we forget to let it out. Play unlocks creativity, shakes off stress and reminds us that life isn't meant to be lived in constant seriousness. Try a new hobby, kick a ball with your kids or sing terribly at karaoke—whatever gets you laughing. When you welcome play back, life feels lighter, as though someone has flung open a window.

Gratitude is the quiet anchor that keeps joy and play steady. It's the practice of pausing to say, "This moment matters." Gratitude doesn't erase hardship—it softens it. Even on messy days, it reminds us there's always something worth noticing: a friend who checks in, the sun breaking through, the comfort of clean sheets. These tiny acknowledgements build resilience, one thank-you at a time.

When joy, play and gratitude become your anchors, life feels freer. Stop measuring yourself by productivity or perfection; measure how alive you feel. Freedom isn't fewer responsibilities—it's carrying them with a lighter heart. So ask yourself: *What if joy were your compass, play your energy and gratitude your anchor?*

7-Day Joy, Play & Gratitude Challenge

You don't need to reinvent your life to welcome joy, play and gratitude back. Small, intentional steps—one each day—can shift your energy and change how you experience life. Think of this challenge as a week-long reset, a gift to yourself. No pressure, no perfection—just a gentle invitation to rediscover the lighter side of living.

- **Day 1: Joy hunt**

  Write one thing that brought you joy today.

- **Day 2: Play break**

  Take 15 minutes for play—game, doodle or dance.

- **Day 3: Gratitude trio**

  List three things you're grateful for.

- **Day 4: Surprise joy**

  Try something new—different walk, new food or a spontaneous "yes".

- **Day 5: Shared play**

  Invite someone into your fun.

- **Day 6: Gratitude note**

  Thank someone who's brightened your life.

- **Day 7: Joyful reflection**

  Reflect on what moments stood out this week.

If a week feels this good, imagine living this way.

Squeeze Your Butt! (A Lesson in Lightness)

Not every step on the journey to joy, play and gratitude is profound—sometimes it sneaks in with laughter. One of those moments came during my personal training sessions, where the workouts led to unexpected life lessons.

I heard this phrase—"Squeeze your butt!"—four times a week. Not whispered over candlelight or shouted at a footy match, but from my Welsh personal trainer while I was red-faced, sweaty and questioning whether burpees were invented as punishment for past-life crimes.

We met during Sydney's lockdowns, when the 5 km rule had us all playing "spot the jogger". A friend suggested that I should train in her backyard. At the time, I was lost in grief after my mum's passing and sinking into depression. I had two options: keep perfecting my couch-potato skills or give it a shot. I chose the latter.

From day one, her bluntness was clear. I joked, "If I collapse mid-burpee, at least you can revive me—you're an emergency doctor." She replied, "Survival rates with CPR aren't very high." Her humour was brutal but laced with care—and it worked. Training in her backyard in freezing winter felt like *Survivor*: the Suburban Sydney special. My nose ran, my hands froze, and I cursed my decision every time I picked up a dumbbell. But I kept showing up. Slowly, the frost gave way to sunshine, and so did my spirit. She even pushed me to enter Spartan and True Grit events—things I'd once thought impossible.

Here's the twist: she never saved me with CPR. She saved me by reminding me of my own strength. Between squats, dumbbells and the god-awful anthem "Bring Sally Up, Bring Sally Down", I rediscovered something I thought I'd lost— lightness. Backyard training became laughter, cheeky banter and proof that I could still play, even while grieving. And that was her gift: the reminder that joy, play and gratitude aren't extras—they're lifelines.

Bringing It All Together: Key Takeaways

Caring for your mind, body and spirit isn't indulgence—it's a necessity. It's the foundation for clarity, resilience and renewal. When you nurture all three, you create steadiness from the inside out. Even small practices, whether laughter mid-training or a quiet note of gratitude, can transform your days.

Through stories and playful challenges, we've seen that lightness often shows up where we least expect it. Strength isn't just muscle—it's humour, connection and the courage to keep showing up.

At its heart, this chapter is about choosing a different compass. Instead of being pulled by pressure and expectation, orient yourself towards joy, play and gratitude as daily anchors. When you do, life feels less like survival and more like full participation—free, light and deeply human. Remember:

- Humour and play aren't distractions—they're medicine for healing and creativity.

- Gratitude reframes ordinary days, showing what's present instead of what's missing.

- Challenges—physical or personal—reveal hidden strength.

- Freedom isn't avoiding responsibility—it's carrying it with a lighter heart.

THE WELSH PERSONAL TRAINER

PLAY & JOY

WHEN MIND AND BODY COLLIDE
EVERYTHING IS POSSIBLE

HEALING ISN'T ONLY ABOUT TREATING THE
BODY—IT'S ABOUT NURTURING THE MIND.
RECOVERY BEGINS WITH THE DESIRE FOR A
BETTER OUTCOME AND THE DAILY CHOICES
THAT SUPPORT IT.

Fatima

YOU CAN'T MEASURE YOUR MOOD IN KILOS OR
YOUR MENTAL HEALTH ON A SCALE.
YOU CAN'T MEASURE THE ENERGY BOOST IN
CENTIMETERS.
YOU CAN'T TAKE A POST GYM SELFIE OF THE
DOPAMINE FLOWING AROUND YOUR BRAIN.
ALL OF THESE HIDDEN THINGS THAT YOU CAN'T
SEE IN THE MIRROR AFTER YOUR WORKOUT ARE
THE THINGS THAT MEAN THE MOST.
TAKE A MOMENT BEFORE YOU COMPARE
YOURSELF TO THE SURFACE LEVEL OF SOMEONE
ELSE ON SOCIAL MEDIA AND THINK ABOUT ALL
THE THINGS THAT RUN DEEPER AS A RESULT OF
MOVING YOUR BODY.
SWEAT CLUB ISN'T A METRIC, IT'S A FEELING -
NOW LET'S SWEAT!

173

Chapter Eleven

Redefining Your Relationship with Money

What comes to mind when you think about your finances? For some, it's stress. For others, it's freedom. Maybe it's the fear of not having enough, the guilt of wanting more or the quiet shame of past mistakes. Perhaps it's the tension between what you earn and what you think you should've achieved by now.

To ease this tension, start small: set realistic goals, celebrate progress and practise gratitude for what you already have. These aren't just milestones—they're stepping stones towards financial freedom.

Here's the thing: we all have a relationship with money. Whether we avoid it, obsess over it, hoard it or spend it like it's on fire, there's a story behind every financial decision we make. And that story is worth exploring.

We often treat wealth like a maths problem, but it's really

a mirror—reflecting our values, fears, self-worth and what we believe we're allowed to have.

Your financial wellbeing—like any meaningful relationship—needs attention and respect. ***Respect means valuing the effort that goes into earning, honouring how you spend and making choices from clarity rather than chaos.*** It means trusting yourself to manage what you have, whatever the amount. Not fear. Not shame. Not worship. Just grounded respect.

In this chapter, I invite you to look beyond the numbers. Let's pause the chase, take a breath and step back from the constant worry about money. It's okay to rest—even in the middle of financial challenges. Let's ask not just how your financial journey looks on paper but how it feels, and how it *could* feel.

Because redefining your relationship with money isn't just about being smarter with your budget. It's about being kinder, wiser and more respectful—to yourself, and to the role money plays in your life.

When the Roadmap Changes: Rethinking Money in a Changing World

Many of us grew up with a roadmap that made sense in another time: study hard, get a "good job", work your way up, buy a home, retire comfortably. But the world has moved on. *So why do so many of us still hold ourselves to rules that no longer fit?*

Technology—especially AI—is reshaping industries at lightning speed. Jobs are evolving or disappearing overnight. Redundancies are no longer rare curveballs; they're part of the professional cycle. People now shift careers multiple times, not because they've failed but because the system itself keeps changing. Add the rise of gig work, short-term contracts and remote roles, and the "traditional" career path looks more like a myth than a model.

Even education is evolving. The pace of change means we can't rely on old qualifications to carry us forward. Self-learning and curiosity—especially in technology and creative fields—are becoming superpowers. They don't just keep you relevant; they give you freedom. The ability to adapt and create multiple income streams shifts you from feeling at the mercy of change to shaping how you thrive within it.

Our definition of success is changing, too. It's no longer just about climbing the corporate ladder or chasing a bigger pay packet. For many, it's about balance, meaning and autonomy. People are taking breaks between roles, upskilling or stepping away from the nine-to-five to pursue something more aligned with their values. Instead of following a straight line, they're building patchwork careers—filled with projects, side hustles and periods of rest.

That shift calls for a new financial mindset—one that supports adaptability, rather than certainty. Adaptability is your key to resilience and confidence in a changing world.

If you've felt out of step with how things "should" be, you're not alone. Your financial wellbeing shouldn't be tied to outdated rules from another era. It should serve you—here, now, on your terms.

My Story

Before we go deeper, let me share a moment from my own journey. It wasn't planned—it came wrapped in uncertainty.

But it taught me more about reinvention, financial wellbeing and clarity than any job ever could.

I was so focused on climbing the corporate ladder that I lost sight of what mattered—until a sudden career change forced me to re-evaluate my relationship with money and success.

I still remember the day my role was made redundant. I was wearing my "I've got this" blazer, with a full calendar of meetings that suddenly, and rather dramatically, were no longer mine. At first, I panicked. I opened my laptop, stared at my CV and considered updating my LinkedIn headline to: *Emotionally available and excellent at Excel.*

But once the shock eased and I stopped measuring my worth by the size of my inbox, I realised this wasn't failure— it was white space. Unexpected, uncomfortable, but full of possibility.

That space gave me room to ask better questions. I signed up for a course I'd been "too busy" for. I took long walks without checking emails. I rediscovered what I enjoyed outside of my job description. I stopped chasing roles that looked impressive and started exploring what felt aligned.

I became more intentional about how and why I wanted to return to the workforce—less about survival, more about purpose.

And in that quiet redefinition, something stirred: *What if I wrote the book I needed when everything felt uncertain?* Writing wasn't part of a career plan—it was part of my healing. I realised I had more to give than performance metrics and polished presentations. I had stories, scars and insights— and those turned out to be more valuable than I'd ever believed. Writing became a way of *reclaiming my voice.*

So, if this chapter finds you in an uncertain season, let me say this: *You are not broken—you are being rebuilt. And brave looks good on you.*

Change doesn't always close doors—it often opens ones we didn't know were there. Redundancy, upskilling and even stepping away from corporate life to carve your own path—these aren't just challenges; they're invitations.

Lean into curiosity and courage, and you'll find that financial wellbeing isn't about clinging to the old roadmap—it's about drawing a new one that finally fits who you are today.

Reflection Box

Questions to ask yourself as you build financial wellbeing in a changing world:

- What "old rules" about work and money am I still holding onto that no longer fit my reality?

- What skills can I acquire to boost my confidence about the future?

- What sparks my curiosity—technology, creativity or new ways of earning—that I could explore now, without waiting for permission?

- How can I diversify my income to feel empowered rather than dependent on one source?

- What does financial wellbeing mean to me in this season—considering not just security but balance and autonomy?

Swipe, Save or Splurge: Decoding Spending Behaviours

When it comes to money, we all fall into patterns—those little habits that show up when we tap our card at the shops, scroll an online sale or say, "Just one more smashed avo toast won't hurt."

These are our spending behaviours. They're not about being "good" or "bad" with money—they're about how we've learnt to feel safe, enjoy life or, sometimes, avoid reality.

Some cling tightly to their savings, while others live for the thrill of spending. Some stick their heads in the sand rather than face their finances. And then there are the jugglers—multitaskers balancing side hustles, contracts or creative projects. Each style has its perks and pitfalls.

The goal isn't to change who you are but to notice your patterns and make minor tweaks so money works *for* you, not against you.

Style	Pros	Cons	Try This
Saver	Always ready for a rainy day. A solid buffer brings peace of mind.	Can miss out on joy in the present. "Someday" often never arrives.	Create a **joy jar**: set aside a small amount for guilt-free treats. Spend it and celebrate!
Spender	Values experiences, generosity and living in the moment.	Buzz fades quicker than the statement in the letterbox. Can slip into debt.	Try the **24-hour pause**: if you still want it tomorrow, go for it. If not, your wallet wins.

Style	Pros	Cons	Try This
Avoider	Doesn't obsess over every dollar. Stays relaxed in the short term.	Minor problems pile up into big ones. Bills don't go away by ignoring them.	Check your account balance while the kettle boils—few minutes, **once a week.**
Juggler	Creative, flexible and resourceful with multiple income streams.	Risk of burnout, inconsistency and chasing too many things at once.	Focus on one **anchor stream** that covers basics, then use side hustles for fun and growth.

From Cents to Sense: How the CARE Puzzle Shapes Financial Wellbeing

By now, you are familiar with the four pieces of the CARE puzzle—and you've probably had a laugh (or a cringe) spotting your spending style. But your style doesn't exist in a vacuum. It shapes, and sometimes shakes, every corner of CARE.

Seeing these connections helps you notice not just how you spend but how it ripples across your wellbeing. When you see the pattern, you can lean into strengths and gently rebalance the rest. Think of it as a mirror—not judgement but *reflection*.

Style	Comfort (Feeling Safe)	Ambition (Growth & Purpose)	Renewal (Energy & Joy)	Equilibrium (Balance & Harmony)
Saver	Strong sense of security; solid safety net.	May hold back from investing in growth or taking risks.	Can neglect fun and self-care in favour of saving.	Stability is high, but it can lean towards rigidity.
Spender	Short-term comfort, but security can be shaky.	Bold in pursuing desires or goals, sometimes without a plan.	Strong on joy, treats and experiences.	Balance is fragile —it can easily tip if overspending happens.
Avoider	A false sense of comfort by ignoring issues.	Growth stalls when financial issues are ignored.	Escapism may feel like joy, but stress lingers beneath the surface.	Lack of balance— minor problems pile up quickly.
Juggler	Comfort is patchy because income can fluctuate.	High ambition, creative and resourceful.	Finds joy in variety and new projects.	Balance is tricky because it carries the risk of burnout or overwhelm.

None of these styles is perfect—and none is disastrous either. The goal isn't to change who you are—it's to bring a little balance into the mix.

Quick Wins for Every Spending Style

- **Saver** → Practise generosity in small ways—shout a mate a coffee, toss a few dollars towards a cause you care about or surprise someone with a little treat. It fosters comfort with letting money flow in and out.

- **Spender** → Keep the buzz but swap the outlet—look for free or low-cost thrills like a gig in the park, a beach day or a community festival. You still get the joy without the dent in your account.

- **Avoider** → Automate the boring stuff—set up direct debits for bills and transfers for savings: that way, progress ticks along even when you'd rather not deal with it.

- **Juggler** → Give yourself a breather—lock in one "no-hustle day" a week where you focus on rest, hobbies or catching up with friends. It keeps burnout at bay and makes your energy more sustainable.

Minor tweaks today can set you up for balance tomorrow.

Every Champion Needs a Coach: Your Finances Deserve One Too

Even the best athletes don't train alone—they have coaches, strategists and guides who help them see the bigger picture. Money works the same way. You can jog along on your own, but having a financial planner is like having a coach who knows the shortcuts and the muddy patches. They're not there to run the race for you but to make sure you don't trip when the pace changes.

A good planner doesn't just crunch numbers—they help you align your finances with your values. They can design a plan that reflects your CARE puzzle and life stage—whether you're saving for a home, juggling school fees, changing careers or preparing for retirement.

Guidance isn't about restriction; it's the key that unlocks options you might not have considered.

Financial freedom isn't about millions in the bank—it's about clarity and confidence. The right planner helps you see money as more than bills to pay. It can fuel ambition, support balance, and let you enjoy life now, not just "one day". Sometimes the bravest move is admitting you don't have to do it all on your own—that's when freedom begins.

Life Stages & Planning

Life Stage	Why It Matters	Planning Focus
Starting Out	Laying foundations for future stability.	Build an emergency fund, consider long-term investments—including pension—early and start good money habits before lifestyle creep kicks in.
Moving in With a Partner	Shared finances can bring surprises and opportunities.	Talk openly about money values, set joint goals, decide how to split expenses and protect your independence with clear agreements.

Life Stage	Why It Matters	Planning Focus
Having a Baby	New responsibilities, new expenses.	Review insurance cover, adjust your budget for childcare and essentials, consider long-term education savings, and explore pension contributions during parental leave (particularly for women, to protect retirement balances).
Between Jobs	Income uncertainty can be stressful.	Protect your savings, tighten your spending, explore upskilling opportunities and consult a planner about bridging strategies.
Life Happens Fund	Life can throw curveballs—illness, caring responsibilities or time off to reset.	Build a dedicated buffer fund; ensure you have life, permanent disability, income protection and trauma cover insurance; and set aside money for essentials so you can plan your next move without panic.
Side Investments/ Hustles	Extra income streams bring opportunity and complexity.	Get advice on tax implications, track expenses clearly and decide how side income supports your long-term goals.
Retirement Planning	Shifting from earning to drawing on savings.	Maximise pension contributions and healthcare plans. Create a strategy that balances lifestyle goals with long-term security.

Take these ideas as general information only—consider your circumstances and speak with a licensed financial adviser.

What Really Matters: Stories of Choosing Meaning Over Status

We often assume the "smart" move is the bigger pay packet or shinier title. But sometimes the bravest—and most rewarding—choices look smaller on paper yet richer in life.

Take Jacinda Ardern, former Prime Minister of New Zealand. In 2018, while serving as the nation's leader, she chose to take maternity leave. It wasn't the obvious career move—it meant stepping back at the peak of her leadership. But she prioritised family, balance and authenticity. She showed that wellbeing isn't only about earnings—it's about choices aligned with values.

Barack Obama's story echoes this. With a Harvard Law degree, he could've taken a corporate role with a considerable salary. Instead, he chose a community organising job in Chicago, earning modestly but gaining purpose. Later, he said those years shaped his leadership. His decision reminds us that financial wellbeing isn't about the size of a pay cheque—it's about the peace of knowing your money and career reflect what matters most.

Both reframed success. Instead of letting money and prestige dictate, they allowed meaning to guide. By choosing alignment over accumulation, they built resilience, fulfilment and clarity. That's the heart of financial wellbeing: money serving your life, not the other way around.

Your worth isn't tied to job titles or promotions. Titles change, companies restructure and industries shift. Your inner compass is what remains. Anchor your financial and career choices to that, and you stop chasing status—you start building a life that feels like yours.

We all meet crossroads: *The job that drains us, or the one that sparks energy and growth? Chasing every dollar, or making space for family, health and creativity?* Choosing meaning doesn't mean ignoring money—it means designing your finances so they support wellbeing in every season.

That choice is always in your hands.

Practical Takeaway Box

Here are three ways to choose meaning without wrecking your finances:

1. **Run the "values check" before the "numbers check".**

   Before saying yes to a job, project or purchase, pause and ask: *Does this align with what really matters to me?* If it doesn't, the dollars won't make it feel right in the long run.

2. **Build a "meaning buffer" into your budget.**

   Just as you'd save for bills or holidays, set aside a small fund that supports meaningful choices—like a short break, extra family time or learning something new.

3. **Think "enough", not "more".**

   Decide what "enough" looks like for your lifestyle and goals. When you know your baseline, you can stop chasing every extra dollar and start using money to support joy, balance and purpose.

Bringing It All Together: Key Takeaways

This chapter reimagined money not as a cold set of bills but as a living relationship—one that mirrors your values, choices and sense of self. We explored how old rules about careers, security and retirement no longer fit today's shifting world, and how adaptability, curiosity and multiple income streams build resilience.

Through my own story of redundancy, we saw how unexpected endings can open space for reinvention, and how respecting money begins with respecting ourselves. We also uncovered how our spending styles—saver, spender, avoider or juggler—shape our wellbeing, and how minor, mindful tweaks can bring greater balance without changing who we are.

Financial planning, as we discovered, isn't just about spreadsheets—it's about seasons. Different stages of life call for different strategies, and the more intentionally we plan, the more freedom and choice we create.

Above all, the heart of financial wellbeing lies in respect and meaning. Treat money as a reflection of your time, energy and values—not as a source of shame or a measure of worth. When you let meaning guide your financial decisions, money becomes a partner in living with clarity, balance and purpose.

In the end, true wealth isn't about how much you earn—it's about how fully your financial choices support the life you want to live.

Chapter Twelve

Next-Level You—Rise, Reset, Reinvent

The phoenix—a mythical bird known for being reborn from its own ashes—never goes quietly. She goes out in flames: scorched wings, sky on fire, ashes swirling in the wind like confetti at her own farewell party. And just when the world thinks she's done, she rises again—not as a copy of her old self but as something wiser, more grounded and unapologetically new.

Now, let's be honest, most of us aren't bursting into flames on a clifftop at sunrise. Our rebirths tend to happen after a quiet breakdown, a long walk in the park with music blasting through our earbuds or a moment of startling clarity during yet another Zoom call that really could've been an email.

Reinvention doesn't require fire, but it does demand truth—the kind that surfaces when you finally slow down enough to hear yourself think. Maybe your old life doesn't fit anymore.

Perhaps you're done apologising for your needs, your voice, your pace. Or maybe you've realised that for all your strength, you've been playing small, and it's time to stretch your wings.

Like the phoenix, your past isn't proof you failed; it's proof you lived, risked and grew. Now, you're ready to rise. Again. And again, if needed. Trust in yourself is the cornerstone of reinvention, that quiet, steady belief that you have the wisdom and strength to find your own way.

It's never too late to become more of who you really are. Reinvention isn't reserved for dramatic moments; it's for anyone brave enough to pause, look inward and ask, *What would a bolder, truer me do next?* Whether you're rebuilding from burnout, boredom or that quiet tug in your chest whispering "not this", remember: you don't need permission to begin again.

You only need the courage to step through the fog, brush off the dust and fly, even if your wings still smell a little toasty. Reinvention is your ticket to freedom: ***a chance to break from the past and step into a future that fits. Embrace that power, and you'll find yourself back in the driver's seat of your life.***

In the pages that follow, we'll explore how to make your reinvention intentional—not just something life throws at you but something you step into with open eyes and an open heart. *Reinvention can be messy, unpredictable, and fuelled by snacks and bold ideas, but it becomes far more powerful when guided by your values instead of fear.*

We'll explore how to shed old labels, tune into your inner nudges and build *You 2.0*—a version of yourself that's aligned, resilient and empowered. It's not about perfection but growth and grace … and a little spark of that phoenix magic that's been within you all along.

The First Step to Reinvention

Recognising the quiet (and not-so-quiet) signals that change is calling.

Reinvention doesn't always arrive with flashing lights and grand exits. Sometimes, it whispers. Sometimes, it nags. Sometimes, it shows up as a slow, aching *meh* that won't go away. We often ignore those signs because change is inconvenient, uncomfortable and uncertain.

But if you pause long enough to really listen, life has a way of letting you know when something new is calling.

The sneaky signals of reinvention

- You feel bored—and you used to care. You're showing up, but the spark is gone.

- You keep saying, "I should be grateful." You are—but you're also suffocating under *fine*.

- You're drained by what once excited you.

- You've outgrown the room you're in—shrinking to fit, laughing at jokes you don't find funny.

- Your body is protesting: headaches, exhaustion, Sunday scaries that start on Saturday.

- You're fantasising about quitting … *everything*.

- You've stopped recognising your own voice— it sounds rehearsed, not real.

- You're constantly distracting yourself— scrolling, snacking, shopping, overhelping.

- You envy people who made bold moves. Not bitterly— curiously.

- You've whispered, "Something needs to change." That whisper is a beginning.

Try this: Circle three of these signals you've felt recently. What might shift if you stopped ignoring them?

Learning to trust the process

Here's the funny thing about trusting the process: it sounds inspiring until it's your life that's unravelling. It's easy to tell a friend over brunch, "Babe, just trust the process," while sipping your turmeric latte, but it's much harder when you're the one hugging a tornado blindfolded.

The truth? Growth is weird. One minute you're journalling about your goals, the next you're crying in the car because you forgot your reusable bags again. And still, somehow, you're growing.

You're becoming. You're learning to be more honest, more grounded and a little less available to nonsense. Trusting the process isn't a single dramatic leap; it's a daily, sometimes *hourly*, decision to keep showing up. It's trusting when you have no proof yet.

Think of it like a Sydney train schedule: confusing, delayed, occasionally rerouted for track work, but still moving.

You might be wondering, *Okay, but what is the process?* It's not a secret map hidden in a dusty drawer or an ancient scroll of wisdom. It's simply small, intentional actions—reflecting, learning, saying no when it matters—repeated until they start to shift how you live, think and feel.

And here's the kicker: ***the power isn't in the process itself.***

It's in you—your willingness to shift gears, to stop waiting for a "better time", to take wobbly, imperfect steps forward.

I don't claim to have all the answers. But I can offer a simple framework, a way to picture what reinvention looks like in real life.

The Reinvention Process: Step by Step

The key isn't speed or perfection—it's honest self-inquiry. The moment you stop avoiding hard questions and start answering them, you begin to change.

To bring this to life, let's look at someone who embodied reinvention: *Coco Chanel*.

What Coco Chanel Can Teach Us About the Process

A story of fashion, freedom and finding your way back to yourself.

Before she was Coco, Gabrielle Chanel was a girl raised in a convent orphanage. No titles. No legacy. She built everything—stitch by stitch, belief by belief.

Her journey mirrored the same steps you can follow today.

1. **Awareness: Snapshot of my now**

   She saw the corsets, the restrictions, the expectations—and asked, "Is this really it?"

   Your turn: What in your life feels like a tight corset right now?

2. **Desire: What's calling me?**

   She wanted freedom, movement, possibility—a life bigger than her past.

   Your turn: What would it feel like breathing freely again?

3. **Needs: Essentials for my becoming**

   She began small—with fabric, courage and belief.

   Your turn: What do you genuinely need to take your next step?

4. **Obstacles: What's keeping me playing small?**

   She questioned every limiting belief society handed her.

   Your turn: Which beliefs are you ready to outgrow?

5. **Strengths: Which thoughts make me unstoppable?**

   Her philosophy: less is more. She trusted simplicity and substance.

   Your turn: What belief helps you walk taller and think clearer?

6. **Knowledge: What's my secret sauce?**

   No degree, but deep intuition and taste. She trusted her eye.

   Your turn: What do people come to you for—even informally?

7. **Assets: What tools are in my back pocket?**

   She used what she had—relationships, creativity, resilience.

   Your turn: What resources are already within reach?

8. **Support: Who are my champions?**

   Mentors, partners and patrons—though not always perfect—were part of her story. Even in times of loneliness, she never pretended she could do it all alone.

   Your turn: Who could guide, support or cheer you on?

9. **Habits: What tiny moves create big shifts?**

   Discipline and consistency built her legacy.

   Your turn: What small daily habit will move your future closer?

10. **Reflection: Who am I becoming?**

    She kept evolving—proof that reinvention never ends.

    Your turn: What are you starting to believe, allow or become?

Coco's story wasn't about fashion. It was about freedom—the kind that begins within.

Starting Again: Two Sides of the Same Brave Coin

Starting again, but with wisdom in your pocket and boundaries in your bag.

It's not about erasing the past. It's about recognising what no longer fits and saying, "This version of me has done its job—now, what's next?"

Starting again is the act.

Reinvention is the intention behind it.

You can start over without reinventing—changing jobs, partners or cities—without shifting the script. ***True reinvention*** *means you change from within. You stop dragging old fears into new beginnings.* You make peace with the past and write the next chapter on your own terms.

Starting again is brave.

Reinvention is conscious.

Together, they make you unstoppable.

Coco Channel's story is proof that reinvention isn't a single event—it's a way of living. And that brings us to the heart of this chapter.

When Starting Once Isn't Enough

A story about real courage—and what it takes to begin again, twice.

When I think about courage, I don't think about grand speeches. I think about my brother.

Yes, I migrated too. I left Venezuela for Australia, where I faced plenty of challenges. *But if I'm being honest?* My journey was a children's game compared to his.

He moved to Chile 10 years ago with his wife and two young children, chasing safety and stability. And while it was safer than what they left behind, it came with its own sting: long hours, low wages and quiet prejudice. They weren't living—they were surviving. And still, they pressed on.

Then the pandemic hit. While most people clung to any security they could find, my brother did something braver: *he let go.* He and his family packed up once again in 2020—this time, they moved to the United States. New country. New system. New struggles. But also, a new chance.

It wasn't easy. But slowly, step by step, they rebuilt. The kids began to thrive at school. They found community. They found purpose. And five years later, they bought a home—not just a house with walls but a symbol of grit, love and the unshakable power of doing hard things twice.

My brother's story reminds me:

Reinvention isn't always glamorous.

Starting over isn't a weakness.

Sometimes, the bravest thing you can do ... is do it again.

Bringing It All Together: Key Takeaways

Start again isn't a single chapter; it's a mindset, a rhythm, a quiet act of rebellion. Whether it begins with a whisper, a collapse or a leap, starting again doesn't mean you've failed. It means you're still evolving. You're still brave enough to admit that beige isn't your colour anymore.

From mythical birds rising in flames to fashion icons defying corsets, to everyday people rebuilding their lives, reinvention is rarely convenient, but it's always powerful. You don't need rock bottom or divine clarity to begin. All it takes is a moment of honesty, a dose of courage and the belief that your future self deserves more than your stuck self of today.

You're not behind. You're simply standing at the edge of your next becoming. So breathe. Rebuild. Wear your ash like a badge of wisdom. And when in doubt, begin again, *bolder*.

- **You don't need flames to rise—just honesty.**

  Reinvention starts the moment you stop pretending you're fine and start asking real questions.

- **Your restlessness isn't a flaw—it's a message.**

  Boredom, burnout, and envy are often your soul's way of nudging you forward.

- **Progress happens one small, imperfect step at a time.**

  Even when you can't yet see the whole picture.

- **You've already done hard things. You can do this too.**

  Courage isn't always loud; sometimes, it's quietly deciding to begin again. Reinvention only works when it's yours.

UNLEASH YOUR PHOENIX POWER

MY BROTHER DARIO, THE MASTER OF REINVENTION

Step One: Awareness
Snapshot of My Now

Step Two: Desire
What's Calling Me?

Step Three: Needs
Essentials for My Becoming

Step Four: Obstacles
What's Keeping Me Playing Small?

Step Five: Strengths
Which Thoughts Make Me Unstoppable?

Step Six: Knowledge
What's My Secret Sauce?

Step Seven: Assets
What Tools Are in My Back Pocket?

Step Eight: Support
Who Are My Champions?

Step Nine: Habits
What Tiny Moves Create Big Shifts?

Step Ten: Reflection
Who Am I Becoming?

THE POWER ISN'T IN THE PROCESS ITSELF. IT'S IN YOU—YOUR WILLINGNESS TO SHIFT GEARS, TO STOP WAITING FOR A "BETTER TIME", TO TAKE WOBBLY, IMPERFECT STEPS FORWARD.

Fatima

One Final Story

My recent trip to Vietnam was an eye-opener. I spent time with locals I met in Vietnam—people who didn't have much in the way of possessions yet seemed to hold an abundance of something far more valuable: *peace*.

Life there moves with a quiet rhythm. People work hard, live simply and carry a deep respect for the world around them. Nothing goes to waste. Every resource has a purpose. Every moment is used with intention. There's a sustainable philosophy woven into their days—one that values balance over excess.

What struck me most was their generosity of spirit. Despite the shadow of a painful past, the locals I met don't dwell on old wounds. They've learnt from their history without passing on the bitterness. "The past should stay in the past," one woman told me with a gentle smile. "We must always look to the future." And they truly do—eyes forward, hearts open.

One day, I joined a local woman in her modest home to learn how to cook traditional dishes. She'd attended an

English course later in life, and that simple act of learning opened doors she had never imagined. It became her bridge to the world—allowing her to connect, teach and share her family's story with travellers like me. Her kitchen was humble but alive with warmth, laughter, and the scent of herbs and hope.

Cycling between villages, I watched artisans create beauty with their hands, families praying for their ancestors' guidance and children laughing barefoot along dusty paths. There was no rush, no noise of comparison—just life unfolding in its natural rhythm.

Vietnam reminded me that a simple life can be rich. That meaning doesn't come from accumulation but from appreciation. And that survival, when met with grace, can evolve into wisdom.

So, the next time you feel stuck or disconnected from what matters, think of them—their resilience, their gratitude, their ability to smile at the future.

Because sometimes, the most profound lessons don't come from chasing more.

They come from learning how to live with enough.

ALWAYS FACE THE FUTURE
WITH A SMILE

EVERY RESOURCE
HAS A PURPOSE

PEOPLE WORK HARD,
LIVE SIMPLY

BECAUSE SOMETIMES,
THE MOST PROFOUND
LESSONS DON'T COME
FROM CHOOSING MORE.
THEY COME FROM
LEARNING HOW TO LIVE
WITH ENOUGH.

Fatima

Conclusion

Here we are—at the end of this book, but not the end of the journey.

If you've stayed with me this far, it means you've done something far greater than reading words on a page: you've given yourself the gift of reflection. You've asked questions that matter, leaned into stories that may have mirrored your own and perhaps even caught yourself wondering, *What if life could feel lighter, freer, more mine?* That curiosity alone is the seed of reinvention.

The first truth this journey has revealed is the quiet power of self-awareness. It's easy to move through life on autopilot, letting old doubts and worn-out stories steer the wheel. But the moment you begin to notice them—really see them—you unlock choice. That slight pause between reaction and decision is where your freedom lives. Self-awareness doesn't ask you to fix everything overnight; it simply invites you to pay attention. And from that attention, new possibilities unfold, placing you firmly back in the driver's seat of your own life.

Alongside awareness comes another essential piece of wisdom: boundaries. For so long, many of us have mistaken boundaries for rejection or feared they'd push people away. But as we've explored here, boundaries are not walls—they're invitations. They say, *This is who I am, this is what I value, and this is how I choose to connect.* They protect our energy, preserve our peace and allow us to give without resentment. Boundaries, it turns out, are an act of love—both for ourselves and for those around us.

Then there's the most practical truth of all: reinvention thrives in the everyday. Big turning points are rare, but small, intentional choices—acts of self-care, play, gratitude and financial clarity—are always within reach. It's the daily dose of you that changes everything. In those tiny, consistent choices, we stop waiting for life to shift and start shaping it ourselves.

Threaded through every lesson is the reminder that reinvention isn't about becoming someone else. It's not about tearing yourself down to start from scratch—it's about returning home to who you already are. Growth adds layers, skills and new chapters, but its essence is alignment: living in a way that feels real and right to you.

And of course, none of this unfolds neatly or in a straight line. You'll revisit old lessons, trip over patterns you thought you'd outgrown and roll your eyes at yourself more than once. But that's not failure—it's progress in motion. Growth is less a straight road and more a spiral staircase; each turn feels familiar, yet each loop takes you higher than before. Every stumble, every repeat, is lifting you closer to clarity.

That's also why humour matters. Reinvention is serious work, but it doesn't need to be heavy. When we can laugh at ourselves—even in the middle of a misstep—we make space to keep going. Laughter reminds us that joy and growth aren't opposites; they're dance partners.

So, what now? My invitation is simple: don't wait for the perfect plan. Choose one small thing that resonated with you here. Maybe it's jotting down your values, saying "no" to something that drains you or finally scheduling that overdue rest day. Start small. Excellence isn't about doing everything—it's about improving, one step at a time.

And remember, you're not walking this path alone. Share your experiments. Tell your stories. Let others see you try. Reinvention multiplies when it's shared—because when you step into your own freedom, you quietly motivate others to do the same. That ripple effect is what everyday leadership looks like, no matter your title.

So, let's not call this goodbye. Think of it as turning the page into your next chapter—one that's already waiting for you. Carry these lessons with you, blend them with your own wisdom and keep writing your story—boldly, playfully, unapologetically.

The world doesn't need you to be flawless. It requires you to be really awake, curious and fully alive.

And as you step forward, may you rise with that quiet knowing in your chest—that you already have everything you need to begin again.

This isn't an ending.

It's your light breaking through.

Thank You for Reading

Reading *Be the Reason You Thrive* suggests a willingness to reflect, recalibrate, and lead with intention — both in life and in work. That choice alone carries weight.

If this book offered insight, reassurance, or a new perspective, I invite you to share your experience by leaving a review on Amazon. Thoughtful feedback helps others decide whether this book may support their own path forward.

More importantly, I hope these pages encouraged you to listen more closely to yourself and to move ahead with clarity and purpose.

I appreciate your time, your openness, and your presence on this journey.

With warm regards,
Fatima Y. Abreu Arellano
CARE TO VOICE Founder

References

Abrams, M. S. (1999). Intergenerational transmission of trauma: Recent contributions. *American Journal of Psychotherapy, 53*(2), 225–231.

Bandura, A. (1986). *Social foundations of thought and action: A social cognitive theory.* Prentice-Hall.

Branden, N. (1969). *The psychology of self-esteem.* Bantam Books.

Branden, N. (1972). *The disowned self.* Bantam Books.

Branden, N. (1994). *The six pillars of self-esteem.* Bantam Books.

Brown, B. (2012). *Daring greatly: How the courage to be vulnerable transforms the way we live, love, parent, and lead.* Gotham Books.

Buqué, M. (2023). *Break the cycle: Healing intergenerational trauma.* Verywell Mind.

Burnett, B., & Evans, D. (2016). *Designing your life: How to build a well-lived, joyful life.* Alfred A. Knopf.

Carpenter, C. (2001). *Create a life of exhilaration and accomplishment in the face of change.* McGraw-Hill.

Clear, J. (2018). *Atomic habits: An easy & proven way to build good habits & break bad ones.* Avery.

Cloud, H., & Townsend, J. (1992). *Boundaries.* Zondervan.

Cohen, S., & Wills, T. A. (1985). Stress, social support, and the buffering hypothesis. *Psychological Bulletin, 98*(2), 310–357.

Crocker, J., & Wolfe, C. T. (2001). Contingencies of self-worth. *Psychological Review, 108*(3), 593–623.

Deci, E. L., Olafsen, A. H., & Ryan, R. M. (2017). Self-determination theory in work organisations: The state of a science. *Annual Review of Organisational psychology and Organisational Behaviour, 4*, 19–43. https://doi.org/10.1146 /annurev-orgpsych-032516-113108

Deichert, N. T., & Fekete, E. M. (2025). Gratitude and physical health. In *The Palgrave Handbook of Positive Psychology and Health* (pp. 73–96). Springer.

Duhigg, C. (2012). *The power of habit: Why we do what we do in life and business.* Random House.

Duckworth, A. (2016). *Grit: The power of passion and perseverance.* Scribner.

Ehrlich, H. (2024, June 16). Success then and now: How definitions have shifted over time. *Innovation, Leadership, Legacy, Mindset, Self-Improvement.* https://holliandrobert.com/success -then-and-now

Erikson, E. H. (1950). *Childhood and society.* W. W. Norton.

Festinger, L. (1957). *A theory of cognitive dissonance.* Stanford University Press.

Frankl, V. E. (2006). *Man's search for meaning.* Beacon Press.

Friedel, R., & Israel, P. B. (2010). *Edison's electric light: The art of invention.* Johns Hopkins University Press.

Gawain, S. (2016). *Creative visualization: Use the power of your imagination to create what you want in your life* (40th Anniversary ed.). New World Library.

Gordon, P., & Robertson, J. (2019). *Spenditude: A life-changing attitude to money.* John Wiley & Sons.

Gray, A. (2010). Confirmation bias – Definition & examples. *Simply Psychology.* https://www.simplypsychology.org

Jans-Beken, L., Jacobs, N., Janssens, M., Peeters, S., Reijnders, J., Lechner, L., & Lataster, J. (2020). Gratitude and health: An updated review. *Journal of Positive Psychology, 15*(6), 743–782.

King, M. L. Jr. (1958). *Stride toward freedom: The Montgomery story.* Harper.

Kirkland, R. (2004). *Taoism: The enduring tradition.* Routledge.

Kübler-Ross, E., & Kessler, D. (2005). *On grief and grieving: Finding the meaning of grief through the five stages of loss.* Scribner.

Maathai, W. (2004). *The green belt movement: Sharing the approach and the experience.* Lantern Books.

McAdams, D. P. (1993). *The stories we live by: Personal myths and the making of the self.* Guilford Press.

Neff, K. D. (2023). Self-compassion: Theory, method, research, and intervention. *Annual Review of Psychology, 74*, 193–218.

Neff, K. D., & Pommier, E. (2013). The relationship between self-compassion and other-focused concern. *Self and Identity, 12*(2), 160–176.

Rand, K. L., & Touza, K. K. (2018). Hope theory. In S. J. Lopez (Ed.), *The Oxford handbook of positive psychology* (2nd ed., pp. 425–442). Oxford University Press.

Ryff, C. D. (1989). Happiness is everything, or is it? Explorations on the meaning of psychological well-being. *Journal of Personality and Social Psychology, 57*(6), 1069–1081.

Shevchuk, N. A. (2008). Adapted a cold shower as a potential treatment for depression. *Medical Hypotheses, 70*(5), 995–1001. https://doi.org/10.1016/j.mehy.2007.04.052

Tawwab, N. (2021). *Set boundaries, find peace: A guide to reclaiming yourself.* TarcherPerigee.

Taylor, P. (2010). *The lazy project manager: How to be twice as productive and still leave the office early.* Infinite Ideas Ltd.

Tracy, B. (2013). *Delegation and supervision.* AMACOM.

Van der Kolk, B. A. (2014). *The body keeps the score: Brain, mind, and body in the healing of trauma.* Viking Press.

Weick, K. E. (1984). Small wins: Redefining the scale of social problems. *American Psychologist, 39*(1), 40–49.

Winch, G. (2013). *Emotional first aid: Healing rejection, guilt, failure, and other everyday hurts.* Hudson Street Press.

About Fátima

Fátima Y. Abreu Arellano is a storyteller at heart and a globally minded professional with a pragmatic edge.

For years, she's helped leaders and organisations design reward and engagement strategies that drive performance while honouring what truly matters: people, purpose and community. Blending lessons from her corporate journey with her own story of reinvention, Fátima shows that authentic leadership begins within.

In her debut book, she invites readers to rise above self-doubt, embrace change with courage, and find the freedom that comes from living and working in alignment with who they really are.

How to Stay in Touch

Thank you for walking this path with me. Writing this book took reflection, courage, and a leap of faith—but knowing it's landed in hearts like yours makes it all worth it.

Connection doesn't end here; this is just where the next chapter begins.

✦ Let's keep the conversation going.

Everything lives in one place— ***www.caretovoice.com***— where I share new reflections, tools, and stories to help you grow and thrive from the inside out.

♥ Join the community.

Subscribe to my newsletter for insights, upcoming events, and personal notes I only send to my readers. Think of it as a gentle nudge of inspiration between life's chapters.

✐ Speaking & Media enquiries.

I speak about emotional clarity, enabling leadership, reinvention, and the courage to lead with purpose and integrity.

If you'd like me to join your next event, workshop, or podcast, reach out at: *hello@caretovoice.com*

💼 Let's connect on LinkedIn.

Join me at *linkedin.com/company/care-to-voice*—where I share ideas that purposefully reshape how we lead, connect, and inspire.

🌐 Social media.

All social media links, event updates, and ways to connect are gathered at *www.caretovoice.com*— it's the best place to start our next conversation.

27581215R00132